Before the Sun Goes Down

Demetrios Trifiatis

inner child press, ltd.

Credits

Author

Demetrios Trifiatis, Ph.D.

Editor

hülya n. yılmaz, Ph.D.

Cover Photograph

Demetrios Trifiatis, Ph.D.

Cover Graphics & Design

William S. Peters Sr.
inner child press, ltd.

General Information

Before the Sun Goes Down
Demetrios Trifiatis

1st Edition: 2023

Publisher Information:
Inner Child Press International
www.innerchildpress.com

ISBN-13: 978-1-952081-96-5 (inner child press, ltd.)

$ 22.95

Dedication

♠ ♠ ♠ ♠ ♠

I dedicate this book to the Divine Light within that which inspires and guides all of us on the path of love, righteousness, and of spirituality throughout life and beyond.

It is only appropriate to remember all the beautiful people that have helped me to grow physically, emotionally, mentally, morally, and academically. Thanks to them, I have been able to compile this humble poetic work and offer it as a thanksgiving to our Lord.

Table of Contents

The Poetry

Muse ~ Inspiration ~ Man ~ Poetry

Table of Contents . . . *continued*

Table of Contents . . . *continued*

Table of Contents . . . *continued*

Table of Contents . . . *continued*

Table of Contents . . . *continued*

Table of Contents . . . *continued*

Table of Contents . . . *continued*

Table of Contents . . . *continued*

Table of Contents . . . *continued*

Table of Contents . . . *continued*

Table of Contents . . . *continued*

Epilogue

The Divine Light Within

Oh, you doubting Man,
don't look at me from afar!
Come closer,
approach me,
examine me,
discover me.

Look, I open up to you.
There is no reason for you
to doubt,
to mistrust,
to be afraid of me.

For

I am the source of light,
the same light that has illumined this world
since the beginning of time,
the same light which is also
enshrined into your soul.

Come nearer.
Do not hesitate any longer.
Respond to my endless calling!

Please,
look more attentively at me,
and you will see the truth,
the only truth:
That
you and I are so much alike!

Preface

Before the Sun Goes Down is my fourth book of poetry, the third solo publication. Its goal is to encourage the reader to understand the world s/he lives in, as well as himself. When they asked Thales, the Greek philosopher of the seventh century BC, what the most difficult thing was for a man, he replied: "To know one's self!"

When Heraclitus, a Greek philosopher of the sixth century BC, was asked, how he achieved wisdom while he never had a teacher, he replied: "I searched within myself!" As we see, both of these two wise men point to the Self, for they know that the self is the microcosm of the cosmic order; thus, they believed the Self to be the door through which Man has to pass in order to understand himself, the Cosmos, and God.

Both philosophers were influenced by the maxim of Apollo, the son of the mighty God Zeus, and the God of fine arts, medicine, music, eloquence, prophecy, and poetry. Apollo's maxim, "Know Thyself" appears to be the way to understand, know, and attain wisdom. Plato (428/427 – 348/347 BC) asserted that our understanding of the world depends on the amount of our experiences and the degree of our knowledge.

This collection of poems represents my experience and my knowledge of the world that I have gained during almost eight decades on this planet. My only wish is to offer this humble book to my fellow humans who aspire to know themselves, understand the world, and get a glimpse of the Divine!

Foreword

This book is written for all those who love poetry and have a special place reserved for it in their hearts. However, knowing the author for over twenty years and being well aware of his academic background in philosophy, I would dare to say that this book is specifically written for people who are thirsty for knowledge and are constantly occupying their minds with eternal questions such as, what is life and what is death. Why are we created and what is the purpose of our existence? Does God exist? What kind of life should we live and why? What is love, friendship, compassion, peace, justice, war, and harmony? How ought we to live and why?

In my view, giving answers to all the questions above, is a Herculean task. It is an impossible undertaking for anyone to handle, unless, s/he turns to the inspiring language of poetry and listens to its whispers. Having realized this fact, Demetrios Trifiatis does exactly what is required: he finds refuge in the language of poetry and he does it brilliantly. The outcome of his decision is this book: *Before the Sun Goes Down.* In it, he offers us his wonderful poetry that enables our soul to escape the bonds of our egos, so as to perceive the world from the higher planes of the spiritual realm.

Every verse and every poem of the author awakes our thoughts and feelings; at the same time, he challenges us to take a stand. He shares, thus, his wisdom, springing out of his rich life experience, including his crossing swords with death on four occasions. The result of his encounters with Hades is a perception of the king of the underworld as his pal, his friend, and not as his foe. “Death”, the author says, “is a celestial pillow upon which the soul rests for a while dreaming of the life to come”. Facing death with equanimity is a sign of wisdom and of acceptance of our mortality, which has as a consequence the minimization and even elimination of our fear of death.

In closing, I would like to say that we are indebted to you, dear Demetrios, for your superb book that makes us intellectually and emotionally richer!

Alexander Helemskii

Professor and Honoured Professor
of Moscow (Lomonosov) State University
Faculty of Mechanics and Mathematics

Introduction

The new book of Demetrios Trifiatis, *Before the Sun Goes Down* shows us that apart from him being a great poet, he is also an outstanding philosopher; a fact that makes him a highly educated individual. This fact, of course, should not come as a surprise to anyone because Demetrios' academic field is that of philosophy; specifically, in Ethics and Metaphysics, which he studied in Canada where he lived, worked, and taught for approximately twenty years. To the above, I would like to add that he also is a charismatic orator; this I know because I have attended some of his presentations that had enriched my knowledge as well as my feelings.

Demetrios' collection of poems in this book touches on a variety of themes that cover all aspects of life: carnal, mental, sentimental, spiritual, and divine. The most important thing for me is that each of his poems carries a specific message and it has a purpose. He wishes to touch our hearts, enlighten our minds and uplift our spirits. He puts emphasis on the moral quality of our life, and although he describes how things are, he always ends up suggesting how things ought to be.

The topics that the author examines are diverse. They start with God and His creation and end with Man and his application of the divine law in everyday life. The values the author supports and highlights in his poems are universal and touch everyone deeply since they concern faith, truth, knowledge, virtue, mercy, compassion, harmony, peace, God, eternity, afterlife, and other universally relevant matters.

Good examples of the effect Demetrios' poems have on the reader are his poems related to death. After having read them, one feels liberated from the fear of dying and thus, considers death as a friend and not as a foe. Whatever form of poetry the author uses, be it Rhyme, Quatrain, Haiku, Personification, Narration, Epigrams, Free Verse, Lantern, Acrostic, Monoku, or any other form, one thing is certain: he always has something meaningful to share in a very gentle and touching way. His heartfelt feelings for humanity and nature, his profound faith in God, his compassion for the needy and the underprivileged, and his adoration of beauty and the divine law fill the reader with warmth, serenity, and understanding.

Dear Demetrios, we thank you so much for your hopeful messages and the uplifting sentiments your poems prompt in us and fill our hearts and souls. Be blessed and continue doing this excellent God-loving work you do!

Maria Fragoulopoulou

Professor Emerita
Department of Mathematics
University of Athens, Greece

The Poetry

Muse ~ Inspiration ~ Man ~ Poetry

Before the Sun Goes Down

Before the sun goes down
Behind the mountains of the temporal
And onto the valley of the eternal,
My soul feels like singing
The sorrows and joys of life
From the dawn of my birth
Till the upcoming sunset of my
Existence!

The Path of Life

Between hope and despair, joy and sorrow,
The path of our life, Thee have traced, my Lord.
So, we live both through good and evil
Before You grant the soul heaven's reward!

A Divine Song

Idle my tongue remained, my Lord,
Till the moment it learned how to pronounce Your name

But . . .

From that moment onward, it never ceased singing your song
Which has set my soul aflame!

Thine Blessings, My Lord

With each breath, I inhale
With each heartbeat, I feel
With each thing, I see
With each sound, I hear
With each flower, I scent
With each being, I touch
With each fruit, I taste
With each step, I take
With each moment, I live
I glorify Thee, my Lord, for all Thine blessings,
The blessings that so many of my fellow men,
The deaf
The mute
The blind
The chronically ill
The invalid
The incapacitated, and
The paralyzed,
Never had the chance to enjoy!

An Ode to Poetry

Oh, poetry,
I so much yearn for
A smile,
A caress,
Or
A kiss of yours,
For
Without your affection,
An empty vessel, my heart remains
Devoid of any feelings, unable
To laugh,
To rejoice,
To love,
While my mind finds it impossible
A single verse to formulate
To glorify the beauty and harmony of
Lord's creation!

Poetry's Mission

Poetry's mission is
To awake the poet who lingers
Within the readers' soul
And to assist him in stretching
The aethereal wings of his imagination,
So as to reach the unimaginable heights
Of perception
From where he would observe reality
From divinity's perspective, hence
Becoming God-like himself!

In God's Hands

From dawn till dusk
And from dusk till dawn,
My life to Thee I entrust, my Lord!

The Divine Symphony

Innumerable times, I have watched
The Sun go down
And as many times, I have witnessed
The calm sea
But
Never have I thanked THEE enough, my Lord,
For me being part of your divine symphony!

Into the Depths of My Soul

Into the depths of my soul, I searched once
The happiest day of my life to find
It was not difficult to locate at all,
For it was the day when God my heart enshrined!

Man's Greatness

A man
Cannot achieve greatness in
The eyes of our Lord,
Unless
Selfless and just he becomes in
His ways!

Regretting the Past

Regretting one's past ruinous actions,
Certainly, is a waste of precious time.
Wise would be to use the lessons learned
To build one's future's edifice sublime!

Accepting Life

I turned
toward my friend, who always was complaining
about the injustices and hardships of life, and in
a calm voice, I asked him:

"Tell me, was there a moment in your life
when you smiled?
Laughed?
Jumped for joy?
Celebrated a success?
Kissed your sweetheart and told her how much you loved her?
Have you embraced your firstborn and exclaimed
how beautiful life is?"

My surprised friend looked at me, took a deep breath, and then
hesitantly, whispered:

"Yes, I have to admit that there were moments like that in my life."

"If there were moments like that, as you have just admitted,"
I continued, "you, certainly, justify each and all of the things
you so vehemently condemned all lifelong!"

My friend looked at me rather confused, saying nothing.
Realizing that there was not to be any reply, I went on:

"You see, my good friend, we humans understand something
only if its opposite exists.
For instance, we understand cold; for, there is warm;
soft because we have experienced hard;
heavy because there is light and so on.

In the same way, we feel pleasure because we have felt pain;
joy because we felt sadness;
happiness because we felt unhappiness.
As you see,
the question is not, how just or unjust life is
but how much we accept life or not accept it.

If we do accept it, we have a chance to be happy.
If we do not, then happiness will elude us.
Therefore, it all depends on the degree
we accept life or not accept it, and
to that degree, we can be either happy or unhappy,
which means, either we would be able to enjoy life
or we would keep lamenting
and complaining about it!"

Thanksgivings to the Muse

Your whispers of inspiration, oh Muse, I heard,
And many verses my elated heart composed.
Now thanksgivings offer my humble book to you,
For your divine poetry has my soul enclosed!

Divine Poetry

Oh, eternal poetry,
The divine language of the Gods
Soul of my soul
Thought of my thought
Breath of my breath
Heart of my heart,
On your enchanting chest,
Let me forever linger.
For, your inspiring heartbeats
I yearn to hear,
So as worthy verses for you
Everlastingly to endear!

A Prelude to the Cosmic Symphony

The prelude of the symphony
of Your creation I heard once, my Lord,
And since then, a note of it I strive to become
with all my heart and mind!

Wondering

I wonder . . .
Is the soul as happy when she leaves the eternal
to be enclosed in the temporal,
as she is when she starts her trip to return
to her celestial home?

I wonder . . .
Whether the enlightened soul is as worried
when she enters the ignorant body,
as she is when she leaves it and has to account
for the success or failure of her mission?

I wonder . . .
Whether the soul is incarnated out of free will
or is she obliged to go through such an adventure, called life?

Finally, I wonder . . .
Whether one day, we would find answers
to these pertinent questions,
either in the physical or in the metaphysical realm?

Till then, my dearest friends,
Let our faith lead the way up to our last breath
with confidence and trust to our Lord's divine plan!

As Above, So Below

Do you know, my dearest friend that
The physical and the metaphysical world are divided
by a membrane only and
they are interconnected and interdependent?

That we, who live on the physical plane, are supervised
by those entities residing on the metaphysical plane?

That we and they both work for the implementation of
our Lord's divine plan, the maintenance of harmony in life?

That the ideas which come to our mind are not our ideas
but they are simply heaven's instructions to us,
inspired by God that we should obey?

That each thought, word, and deed of ours must aim at the
universal good and not at our interest?

That whatever we think, say or do, doesn't go unnoticed
but is recorded by heaven and follows our soul
wherever it goes?

That the paramount command we ought to follow is
to love one another?

That whoever loves his friend as he loves himself,
loves God and God loves him?

If you do not ignore these truths, my friend, then a blessed soul
you would be here and in the hereafter!

Sailing Over Life's Ocean

My life's ship,
Under the watchful eye of The Lord,
Opened its adventurous sails of hope and
Prepared to cross
The turbulent ocean of afflictions without fear,
Searching for the harbor of tranquility
That God has prepared for it to anchor!

I Wonder, If Ever a Day Comes . . .

I wonder,
If ever a day would come
When you and I, my friend,
Would refer to ourselves not
As American, Asian, or European;
As black, yellow, or white;
As Christians, Muslims, or Buddhists;
As friends or foes,
But simply as brothers,
Inhabitants of this planet
Who care and love one another,
United under the flag of humanity
With one nationality,
One religion,
One God?
. . .

I just wonder!

Musings: Do Not Wonder

Wise people know that they know nothing.
Erudite people doubt that they know many things.
Ignorant people are certain that they know everything.

Now,
The first category of people refuses to rule, and
The second is reluctant to do so.
It remains in the third category to govern the world.
Therefore, do not wonder, my friend,
Why we find humanity in such a mess!

Patience

Patience
Is the wise charioteer that holds the bridles of the impetus
To guide us safely over the hurdles of recklessness and haste!

Forging One's Character

Necessity
Is the anvil upon which
Destiny forges one's character
By using the hammer of life's afflictions
According to divinity's will!

The Real Me

I was put on the road of life without my consent.
I was not conscious of who I was or of what I had to do and
What direction I should go.

I was just asked to follow in the footsteps of my predecessors who
Dressed me the way they were dressed,
Baptized me into their religion, and taught me,
Their language
Their history
Their tradition, and
Their culture.

On the way, they also indicated to me
Whom to trust and whom not to trust,
Who my friends and my enemies were,
Whom I should love and whom to hate.
Thus, before I became an adult and formed my own opinion about
The nature of persons and things,
I already had become one of them.

Growing older though, and being educated under different systems,
I started questioning the correctness of the values and ideas with
Which I was brought up.
Thus, I asked myself:
Is my religion really “my” religion?
Are my enemies really “my” enemies?
Are my friends really “my” friends?
Are my values really “my” values?
Are my ideas really “my “ideas?”

If they are, then there is no problem,
But if they are not, then, who am I?
Who is the real me?

To give answers to these questions, I had to reinvent myself.
I had to see me, not through the prism of their
Education,
Religion,
History,
Tradition, and culture,
But through my own prism,
The newly discovered prism of my "pure" self;
The self that was liberated from all the prejudices of the past;
The self that saw the world I lived in
Under a new light of understanding,
The light of my universal self;
The self that didn't belong to a race, a creed, or a nation,
But to humanity, to love, to the universal brotherhood,
And to God.

To achieve this, though,
I had to put myself into a parenthesis;
A parenthesis that helped me withhold for some time
All my judgments
Till I decided what ideas I will accept and what ideas I will refuse;
Whom I will trust and whom I will mistrust,
Whom I will love and whom I will hate.

When this introspection and reevaluation were completed,
Then and only then was I able to present myself to the world;
Then and only then was I able to shout at the top of my voice:
"Here I am, my brothers, my sisters! This is the real me!"

Glorifying God

Each time I see
The golden sun
The silver moon
The platinum stars
        I see Thee, my Lord!

Each time I hear
The rain to fall
The brooks to murmur
The falls to roar
        I hear Thee, my Lord!

Each time I touch
The morning dew
The blooming flowers
The tender leaves
        I touch Thee, my Lord!

Each time I scent
The flower's aroma
The air's fragrance
The sea's saltiness
        I scent Thee, my Lord!

Each time I taste
The ripened fruits
The sweet honey
The intoxicating wine
        I taste Thee, my Lord!

Thou art
The source of my life

The reason for my being
The cause of my thoughts
The ruler of my feelings
The savior of my soul.

Without Thee, there is
No meaning
No purpose
No grace
No salvation.

Thus,

Eternally,
I would worship Thee, my Lord, and shall
Devote my life to serving Thee in all humility,
Claiming nothing for myself,
Glorifying Thee with every thought, word, and deed of mine
In the best way I would be able to,
In the hope that I could help others
The way Thee would like me to do!

One or the Other

No, my friend,
We are neither pure good nor pure evil.
We are both good and evil!

Look
At all these pairs of opposite forces below:
Hope and fear
Courage and cowardice
Success and failure
Pleasure and suffering
Happiness and unhappiness
Knowledge and ignorance
Virtue and vice
Love and hate.

They are all coexisting in one's soul in perfect harmony
Till the moment we are called upon a decision to take
Then, a vicious war of domination begins
Between the opponents
That usually lasts a lifetime,
And pending who the winner of this conflict is,
We, my beloved friend, become one or the other!

The Kingdom Within

You, my friend,
Are not a king or a prince,
Neither are you a nobleman
Of a higher or lower rank,
You are just another poor man like me:
A citizen of perpetual want.

Yet

You carry within your heart a kingdom,
A kingdom, you very well could inherit
With God's grace
If only Lord's divine Word you choose to
Listen to and follow virtue's path He indicates!

Infusing Love

If we infuse love into our children's hearts
And teach them respect for all nature and life,
Soon, many more things for peace we would achieve
That would end humanity's destructive strife!

The Solemn Knights of Light

Do not despair my friend,
There is still hope for a better world
For us to make:
Kinder,
Nobler, and
More just.

I discern
Far on the horizon of time,
The dawning of a new era,
An era of love and understanding.

Look,
There is the cavalry of the righteous,
All set up to mount their horses of virtue.

Now,
I clearly see them –
These solemn knights of light,
Ready to gallop on the fields of
Universal brotherhood
With their swords of retribution
In hand to overthrow evil's empire of hate and
Enthrone our Lord's fallen law of love,
Restoring it to its previous glory.

Thus, bringing, at last, peace on earth,
The peace for which our heavenly father
Has his only son sacrificed!

Shareholders of Good and Evil

We are all shareholders of good and evil,
Since in this world, we share the same.
Though, the dividend of the good we rush to cash in,
The dividend of evil we leave unclaimed,
Hoping someone else would show up to cash in
And take the blame!

Nature's Secrets

Listening attentively to nature's whispers,
The secrets of eternal life, I was taught
Secrets, hidden in every being, existing
That my perplexed mind forever has them sought!

As Enemies, We Were Never Born

No, my loving friend,
As enemies, we were never born but we were made
By all those evil men who had the most to gain.
Thus, I implore you, be ready each other to embrace,
Forgetting to which religion we belong and to what race!

Serving Humanity

Only when one finds the courage
To sacrifice his ego
On the altar of love,
Then, and only then,
Can he be ready to devote himself
Into the service of humanity!

Becoming Wise

Becoming wise, my beloved friend,
There is a thing that we all ought to know:
We have to accept our ignorance before the Lord,
Wisdom on us will He bestow!

Morality

Morality is mainly
The product of compassionate acts
That are inspired by the divine,
Supervised by wisdom,
And applied by love!

Life's Miracle

Life . . .
This drama
This mystery
This enigma
This paradox
This choreography
This symphony
This phantasmagoria
This poetry
This ecstasy
This apotheosis of creation

Is

The greatest demonstration of
God's existence and might,
Whose wisdom brings together spirit and matter
Within Man's soul;
Thus, guides and enables him to achieve
Cosmic awareness, and become a
God-like figure himself.

For

The glorification of his Creator
And the establishment
Of His divine law are upon our planet!

Let Us Love

If

There is anything worth
Dying for, my friend, it is
LOVE:
Love for our God
Love for our country
Love for our family
Love for our friends
Love for our fellow Man
Love for love's sake,

Because

There is nothing nobler,
Nothing more dignified
Nothing more elevated
Nothing more holly
Nothing more sacred,

Since
Nothing is more divine than
Love.

For love

Is God's voice
Is God's will
Is God's wisdom
Is God's determination to unify
The Cosmos and Man alike,
And by doing so, to make both of them whole!

Therefore

Let us love my friend
Let us love unselfishly
Let us love unconditionally
Let us love altruistically
Let us love compassionately
Let us love benevolently.

For

That is the only way
For the anxiety of Man for human affairs
Forever to disappear, and peace and harmony
To be established on our planet and in our souls!

God's Reflection

In truth, my dearest friend,
Each one of us is intended to be the reflection of
God's wisdom and goodness.
Unfortunately,
Not all of us are willing or able to polish the mirror of our soul
Upon which His righteousness and knowledge may be reflected.
Thus, in many cases, His holy image is distorted
Due to our inability
To follow His path of Light!

Afflictions

The afflictions we may face in life
Are not to be seen as punishments,
But as valuable lessons to be learned
By all those who seek wisdom!

Wisdom's Temple

If you, my friend,
Aspire wisdom's temple to build,
Be patient and, in silence, the cornerstone of it lay
Self-knowledge!

The Torchbearers

Although God shows no favoritism to any soul –
For each soul is a part of Him,
He is delighted to respond to any man's plea for
Light
Truth
Virtue,
Justice, and wisdom,
Since God knows that these men
May become the saviors and torch-bearers
Of love
Of mercy
Of compassion, and
Of humanity!

Wisdom's Lovers

Advisable would be for someone,
Who endeavors wisdom to attain
To seek Socrates' rebukes,
Rather than the applauds of fools to claim!

Life's Lesson One

Geniuses are after Wisdom.
Clever people are after Knowledge.
Fools aren't after anything.

For

Fools think they know everything;
Thus, spend their time criticizing
Everyone and everything!

The Finest of Wines

Yes!
At the top of my voice, I confess that
Intoxicated I am by life's unsurpassed beauty;
For its finest wine I have drunk:
God's love!

Drops of Wisdom

Drops of wisdom fell
On ignorance's arid ground.
Understanding sprang!

One Tongue Only

Fortunately, the Lord, in His infinite wisdom,
Has given us only one tongue to express ourselves,
What our eyes and ears witness every day.

If He had given us two tongues,
Multiple would have been the confusion
And easier for the world to go astray!

Your Love, My Lord

Your love, my Lord,
Is the fortress of my soul that
No enemy of your Word
Would ever be able its walls
To ascend
To establish, the realm of hate!

A Melodious Tune

My soul is humming a melodious tune of
Gratitude, love, and affection
For all my beloved and caring friends,
Who offered prayers for my health's restoration.

The battle was fierce, and the enemy ever so furious,
But he was defeated, no matter the methods he did apply.
For, whoever fights with God on his side,
Doubly armed he is.
For, with faith, his strength does multiply!

* After a nasty fall, a large brain Hematoma was formed, which brought me close to death.

Love's Blooming

If we all let love bloom in our hearts,
Humanity shall be beautified.
If the Word of our Lord we'll follow,
His holy name shall be glorified!

Sacrificing Self-Interest

Oh, empathy,
You, divine child of love,
I implore Thee to help us sacrifice our self-interest
On the altar of the common good.
For, only in this way, mankind could put aside
Their differences and find solutions
For the benefit of us all!

The End of Wars

The wise, I asked the other day, my friend,
When the wars among nations would end.
He looked at me with pity and replied,
"When love with justice in Man's heart would blend!"

The Cosmos, the Flower, and the Bee

Look as far and as wide as you can, my friend,
Turn your eyes towards the sky and try to pierce infinity –
This vast unknown.
Ponder about its existence.
Let not a single thing unexamined,
Any stunning flower untouched,
Any majestic bird unobserved,
Any magnificent fish unnoticed,
And tell me: Isn't life a miracle?
An unbelievable story?
An inconceivable design,
Yet, a mesmerizing reality?

Look at how heaven and earth are put together:
A harmonious whole operating with such precision and
With a single purpose in mind: LIFE!

Tell me, could this great design be the outcome of chance?
Of hazardous consequences?
Or was it the work of blind forces?

Look closer my friend, once again,
Pay attention to the details of this incredible miracle of life.
Look how things are so wisely operating.
Observe the relationship between a flower and a bee,
How they are interrelated,
Interconnected and
Interdependent.

Marvel how, although they both are so transient,
They maintain eternity.

Note the way they obey the cosmic laws,
Thus, enacting the choreography of life and death
That divinity has conceived;
And by doing so, they become divine themselves
And their art holy.

Let us, my friend,
Be inspired by them and let us create our own
Harmonious coexistence,
Our own choreography, inspired by God
To incarnate His will in reality,
So as to glorify His creation
And for us to live in peace as He meant us to live!

The Road to Knowledge

For the one who wastes much time wandering
Through the dark alleys of disbelief,
The road of celestial knowledge is
Bound to be missed!

A Man's Character

As a musical instrument is judged
By the quality of the melody it produces,
So is a man's character judged
By the thoughts, words, and deeds he induces!

Weapons of Peace

Let us, my friends, create the most powerful weapons of peace,
Weapons that would surpass in force all those that war possesses,
Able to carry to every heart reason, compassion, and love
So as the entire world on humanity's path progresses!

Good Over Evil to Prevail

When I was young,
The future stretched endlessly before my bewildered eyes,
Reaching as far as the horizon of infinity;
Thus, making me feel invincible and immortal.

Life was an enjoyable experience for me back then.
At every moment, she was revealing to me,
One after the other,
Her many marvels.

No surprise that I was infatuated with life's beauty
And her many challenges.
So, when I was invited to follow her adventurous ways,
I did not hesitate at all.
On the contrary, I rushed forward and
Became one of her actors on the central stage.
Thus, I turned into her most enthusiastic devotee.
So, I dared to dream to change the world:
To fight the evils that made societies suffer
To eradicate hate
To obliterate wars
To eliminate hunger
To establish justice
To bring peace, and
To irrigate the tree of love in Man's heart.

For decades, I gallantly fought against good's formidable
opponents, but to no avail.

Time has passed, and as I approach the closure
Of my eighth decade, I am not anymore, an actor
On the central stage.

I have become one of the innumerable spectators of it,
With no strength to keep up the struggle.

Now, I can only pray.
Pray to God to send fresh troops that are
More courageous than I
More daring
More determined
More unafraid
For the final victory to be achieved
And for good over evil to prevail!

Life ~ Man ~ Destiny ~
~ Peace ~ War ~ Justice ~
~ Good ~ Evil ~ Age

Destiny and Us

We had better follow our destiny, my dear friend, to where it may.
Otherwise, she would drag us without our consent along the way!

Revealing Our Destiny

If one wishes to see his destiny,
One should not look at the stars to find a reply.
For, all answers to everything that in one's life may occur
Deep down in one's own heart lie!

A Wonderful Adventure

Life, a wonderful adventure it could be,
If we, unselfishly, love ourselves and
Care for others!

A World of Peace and Love

Tell me,
My dear friend,
My beloved brother,
My trusted ally,

Till when are we going to let
The autocrats
The dictators
The despots, and
The tyrants govern us?

Till when do we intend to allow these
Barbarous
Vicious
Immoral, and
Unholy glory-seekers rule our lives?

Till when are we going to permit these ignorant monsters
To imprison
To torture
To maim, and
To kill their own people?

Till when are we going to observe these savages
Attacking,
Occupying
Enslaving, and
Obliterating smaller nations?

For how many more millennia
Do we have to witness the devastation

Of humanity because of these morally impotent criminals
Who instill tons of hatred in the hearts and minds
Of our fellow humans?

Tell me, my friend, my brother, my trusted ally,
Isn't it about time to revolt against such malicious rulers?
Against such practices?
Against war?
Against ignorance, and
Against injustice?

Has not the time come to replace these bloodthirsty evil men
With virtuous men?
With men of a loving heart and mind?
With knowledgeable men?
With compassionate men for peace?
With men of wisdom and justice?

Come now, my fellow human,
I wish you would agree with me.
Please agree with me. I beg you to agree with me.
I implore you to agree with me if you, too, wish to see
A fellowship of men and nations that care for each other
And is kinder,
Nobler, and more loving.
Otherwise,
The afflictions of humanity will never end;
Unless, as Plato has indicated in his *Republic*,
The wise and the just would rule the world
Or those who rule the world
Become just and wise!

Braving the Storms of Life

Those who brave the storms of life
Taste in full the essence of it,
While those who seek shelter to find,
Ignorant of life's thrills, forever, stay!

When Grief Plows Your Heart

When relentless grief plows your heart,
And intolerable is the pain
Forget not to sow your dream's seed.
At harvest, you would know your gain!

Obeying Time's Decree

I salute you oh, mighty Time:
My best friend,
My worst enemy,
For to live without you is simply
Unimaginable!

Throughout my existence,
I have, unsuccessfully, struggled to accept
Whatever you brought to me.
Either it was a sweet smile
Or a bitter tear with equanimity.
Since I could not enjoy the one
Without suffering the presence of the other.
This, you told me, is the order of things,
This is what the heavens decree;
But I, a fool ignorant, resisted.
Now, however, older and wiser,
An obedient child of yours, oh, Time,
I have finally become
So as to abide by your universal rules
Of growth and decay,
Without my lips,
A single complaint to pronounce!

My Life's Breathing Account

Each day, breaths withdraw
From my life's breathing account –
My balance . . . unknown!

Fighting Against Evil

Evil should be attacked in its infancy,
Otherwise, difficult it would be to confront it
When it reaches adulthood!

The Privilege

I started the day
The way thousands of days I have
Started before.

The sun had barely risen above the horizon.
It seemed to hesitate for a while, then climbed higher,
Determined was he to chase away
The remaining shadows of the night!

I stood there in silence,
Observing and admiring this magical phenomenon,
Pondering,
How lucky and grateful I am to be still here,
Living,
Thinking,
Feeling,
Loving,
Wondering, and
Dreaming of the future.
Suddenly,
My mood changed.
It became somber, then turned gloomy
As I thought of all those people
Who, during the night, had lost this privilege that
We enjoy now:
To be alive!

*In memory of the thousands of our brothers and sisters around the world who lost the battle against COVID-19 last night! R.I.P., for a greater privilege than ours waits for you in heaven!

Beware of the Beast

We all pride ourselves because we live in the year 2023,
A year in which humanity so much progress has done.

Violence and hatred . . . we thought were things of the past,
And war and terror, we believed, were not possible to last.

Then a moment comes, when an appalling act takes place
That makes all of us look ourselves in the face.

Then we realize with much horror and a lot of disgust
That the beast Man carries within may turn the world to dust!

Chaos, and Harmony

In the beginning, there was Chaos,
Hesiod of Old tells us.
Then, with the passing of time and the intervention of the divine,
Slowly and persistently, the order was established.
But Chaos has not disappeared at all, as it is lurking
Around the core of Cosmos –
Around every heart
Around every mind, and
Around every soul,

Waiting for the right moment to strike, and
To overthrow harmony and back to anarchy
To us, triumphantly, to bring.

Imperative it is, therefore,
With each step we take,
Vigilant to be, my friend,
Questioning everything that concerns us –
Our being
Our dreams
Our becoming.
Thus, advisable for us would be
Never to accept something at
Its face value.

On the contrary, we should examine in depth
Everything that concerns us.
So, advisable would be, suspicion's shield high to raise
To protect our inner order that we have so painstakingly achieved.
By doing so, victims to Chaos, we would never fall!

Good and Evil

You and I, my friend, are not different at all, although
At first glance, we seem to come from very different worlds.

True, you wear the regalia of justice, virtue, and love
And I, the rugs of injustice, vice, and hate,
But don't let yourself be deceived by appearances, though;
For we are the descendants of the same father: Eros or Cupid.

As you may know,
Eros was the child of the goddess Aphrodite
Or Venus, the Goddess of Love,
And that of Ares or Mars – the God of War
Who apparently are our grandparents.

It is clear, therefore, that you are not just my friend
But rather my brother.
For, whatever characteristics we both have inherited,
Are the results of their sacred union.
Thus, the virtues inherited by you, I have inherited them as well,
And the vices that you see in me
Are also to be found in your soul.

From that we easily could conclude that you are not born
Intrinsically good, nor was I born intrinsically evil.
Only the decisions we take and the choices we make
In the circumstances life puts into us makes the difference.

We must remember that there is nothing purely good
Or purely evil, for the two forces coexist
And the two are interconnected.

Needless to say, then, that I could very well be you and you,
Very well be me if you and I had differently acted.

You see, my brother,
Necessity has established within our souls a divine strife –
This endless battle of Venus against Mars, each of them aims
To gain supremacy in the core of our being.

Now,
Pending who the winner of this titanic struggle is,
Determines who is going to be declared good
And who is going to be declared evil!

The Tiny Creature

There it is,
On the screen of my mobile phone,
A real tiny creature, advancing from one corner of
The phone to the other.

I observe this microscopic living thing:
A tiny head
A tiny body
Tiny legs that are almost invisible, but
Still, they help the creature advance.

I wonder . . .
What is it? Where does it go?

Unfortunately, I have no answers to give.
So, a mystery to me this creature remains.
I even ignore its name, or even wonder if it has a name.
Nevertheless, whatever it is, it parades before my very eyes,
Surprising me
Puzzling me
Confusing my mind.

What is it?

An enigma certainly for me it remains.
But whatever it is, there is no doubt that it is God's creation
And as such, for sure, it has
A purpose in life
A goal to achieve
A mission to accomplish,
A mission, no less important, to the eyes of the Lord, than mine.

For, we both come from the same source.
Thus, we both are as much divine.
Consequently, we both work to complete
God's holy design!

Getting Older: A Reason to Celebrate

"How old are you, Professor?"
I turned around, trying to locate the student who had asked this unexpected question.

It was not hard to locate her. There she was, smiling, her hand up in the air.
"I am forty-two," I replied. "Why?"
"Would you like to be my age?" She continued.
"How old are you, my dearest?" I inquired.
"Nineteen!" She answered.
I looked her straight in the eyes and emphatically declared:
"Of course not!"
"Why not, Sir?" Shouted, almost all the students in the auditorium, as they were taken by surprise.

Since I had their attention, I thought it a good opportunity to talk to them about age, although I had nothing prepared.
I turned to the student who had asked me the question In the first place, and asked her again:
"How old did you say you are?"
"Nineteen."
"Would you like to die today?"
She looked at me, rather puzzled by my question, but she firmly replied:
"No!"
"What about tomorrow?"
"No!"
"In a week, perhaps?"
"No!"
"In a month, a year, in five years?"
"Certainly not!"
"What about ten or twenty years from now?"
"Absolutely, not!"

"You see, my dear student," I said: "You are dreaming of
becoming my age."
"It seems so!" She timidly replied.
"I wish you to reach my age and to live to be one hundred years
old, but are you sure you are going to live to be forty-two?"
"Honestly, I do not know." She whispered.
"Let us say, that you will reach the age of forty-two,
could you tell me if you would be healthy, and have two legs,
arms, and eyes? Have a career, a family of your own as I have?"
I asked.
"No, Sir. I do not know if I will."

I paused for a while and observed my students who had become
very interested in the dialogue and added:
"You see, my dearest student, you are a potentiality
but I am a reality. Why would reality ever wish to become
potentiality again?"

Then, I went on to mention that in the Greek language the word "old" (Geros) means the "privileged one" because an old person is considered to be favored by fate. Therefore, getting older should be a reason to celebrate, rejoice, be grateful and happy, and not be gloomy, miserable, and unhappy.

"Remember, my dearest students," I continued, "getting older is
the only way for us to stay alive."
Then, in a teasing mood, I asked:
"Would you like to be my age?"
"Yes, Sir. We would!" Was their reply, and they burst out into
laughter!

*This poem portrays a true story.

The Inscription

Finally,
What I wished for came to pass.
After many decades of a turbulent life, I managed to reach
The gates of old age!

Now,
Before them, I stand,
Pondering at the inscription written above the entrance:
"Enter at your own risk!"

One Nation

I see a day far into the future,
When the whole planet a single nation shall be
Where people would care for one another
As we care for ourselves today, you and me!

Raising Children

Raising children
Is the loftiest and bravest of human endeavors, for
It requires a life filled with
Constant battles,
Ceaseless agonies, and
Perpetual sacrifices,
Without ever knowing, if the efforts made will be
Crowned with success!

Getting Older

Oh, my fellow mortals,
Shouldn't we stop complaining about getting older
When we very well know that it is the only way for us
To stay alive?

Silence Is Not Always Golden

Silence is golden, they say.
To that, in many cases, I all heartedly concur,
But one should never stay quiet
Whenever one witnesses an injustice occur!

Good Fortune, Bad Fortune

Fortune,
Whether good or bad, doesn't discriminate between
The poor and the rich
The powerful and the weak
The young and the old,
For, like an infatuated maiden,
She comes and goes as she pleases,
Without ever giving any warnings, offering any explanations
Or feeling any regrets,
As she knows very well that in a cyclical world of becoming
Nothing is permanent.
Thus, what appears today as a good fortune
May lead to the greatest misfortune tomorrow and . . .
Vice versa!

Life's Sacred Nectar

Youth, a temporal ladder it is, that
Might help one climb onto the plains of old age
Where the fruits of experience and learning are ripe,
Allowing him to relish life's nectar and to become a sage!

Life's Secrets

Once, I asked mysterious life
All her secrets to reveal.
Since I didn't get any reply,
Her lips . . . I had to unseal!

The Holiest of Temples

Every woman is
A temple of God's love.
However, when with a child,
She becomes the holiest of the temples.
For, the Divine Will of our Lord
Does incarnate.
Thus, an imperative it is for us,
Her to venerate!

Pity Not the One

Pity not the one whose path is littered
With broken dreams

But

The one who dreams of a companion had
None on his way!

Confronting My Destiny

My destiny,
I confronted fiercely the other day,
Complaining about the many obstacles
She has placed before me on my path,
Plus, for all the calamities and pains
That she has so mercilessly inflicted
Upon me.

She heard my protests with disdain,
But with them, she didn't agree.
Then she angrily retorted,
That the blame should not be put on her,
But rather upon me,
Since once she had heard me exclaim:
"How beautiful, in reality, can life be!

Possible, Impossible

When I was young, oh, life,
The breeze of your dreams gently caressed my
Enchanted, innocent heart,
Making me believe that all I wished for was within
The reach of the Possible.

With the passing of unforgiving time, though,
And the coming of the inescapable old age,
Plus, the scourging sun of merciless reality
Evaporated my youth's illusion:
Of Impossibility's nonexistence!

Rarer Than Diamonds and Gold

Although Virtue and Justice,
Rarer than gold and diamonds have become,
Man ought to never give up going after them
If he wishes his links with the divine to keep
And his humanity to maintain!

A Particular Species

Oh, what a particular species we humans are!
At the moment we spend our evanescent life,
Undermining the moral foundations this world is built on,
Just for a temporal gain, we kneel before the Eternal
When things go wrong,
Imploring the Lord to deliver us from anything
That causes pain,
Forgetting, that in most cases, we are the ones,
Who deserve the blame!

Impossible

Humanity, no matter how hard it tries,
Would never manage in perfect harmony to live.

For,

There always would be some evil people
Who would deny harmony any chance to give!

The Smiling Death

As the clock of war is loudly ticking,
Broader the smiles of death become.
For the passing away of souls is thinking
Onto the oblivion's horrific land!

Ukraine

The hyenas of war are unleashed
The carcass of freedom to devour.
The entire world is holding its breath
As, in awe, it watches Ukraine's last hour! *

Weeping Angels

Clear was Ukraine's sky.
  Drops of rain started to fall . . .
    Angels' bitter tears!

* Both poems are dedicated to all the innocent victims of Ukraine's war.

Toothless and Blind

You killed one of mine.
I killed two of yours.

You retaliated, killing ten of my brethren.
I hit back, killing one hundred of your people.

Enraged, you eliminated thousands of my countrymen.
Outraged, I obliterated a town of yours.
To get even, you destroyed a city of mine!

I came back . . .!

The same thing is repeated for thousands of years:
An eye for an eye, and a tooth for a tooth!

And now here we are, my enemy,
Both with one eye
And both, with few teeth left.

Don't you think
That the time has come for us
To end this insanity
Before we end up both
Toothless and blind?

The Heavenly Way

The shadows of doubt were following me since my life's dawn,
Overcasting my thoughts so as not to find the place
Where I belong.

But You, my Lord, have shown me Your everlasting
Heavenly way:
To love every being of your creation
Unconditionally to this day.

For that, my heart, incessantly, Your glory would gratefully sing,
Continuously working for the desired peace
Onto this planet to bring!

Nature ~ Man ~
Environment ~ Life ~ God ~
Climate Change ~ COVID-19

God's Guests

We are nothing but the guests
To whom God has extended His hospitality.
Thus, we ought to be guarding and
Revering nature's sacred universality!

Dancing to Nature's Tune

To live in harmony with nature,
Man has to learn to dance to the sound of
Her music of collaboration,
Of interdependence,
And of harmonious coexistence!

Have You Ever . . .?

Have you ever exclaimed, my friend,
"How beautiful is life!"
When you gave your first kiss to your beloved?
Married your sweetheart?
Took into your arms your firstborn?
Had great success in life?
Or when you admired the beauty of nature?
Scent the aroma of a flower?
Enjoyed one of Beethoven's symphonies?
Cried while listening to an opera?
Saw your most cherished dream come true?

If

You have ever uttered these four words, my fellow mortal,
No matter what the reason was that made you do so,
Then without fail you have justified
All impediments,
All grief,
All suffering,
All agony, and all pain
That life has put or will put in your way!

Spring's Artwork

A cascade of poppies,
Caressing ecstatic ground –

Spring's composition.

May's Laughter

Smiling seeds sprout fast.
The giggling ground welcomes their roots –

May bursts out laughing!

Spring's Glory

Spring's coronation

    Roses' celebration

        Beauty's exaltation:

            MAY!

Nature's Wondrous Gown

Autumn . . .

Nature's wondrous gown,
Weaved by leaves of myriad hues
As they dance on the branches,
Listening to the melody
Of the enchanting wind!

Earth's Agony

Earth's agony mounts,
Humans augment their demands –

Life . . . its last breaths count!

The Land's Future

Icebergs are melting.
The sea level is rising fast –

Bleak is the land's future!

The Wisdom of the Cosmic Order

Thoughtlessly, the Unwise, spends his time,
Criticizing the works of heaven's coder
While the wise never lets a moment pass without praising
The infusive cosmic order!

The Love of God

No matter what,
The love of God for Man is given
But Man should know that ruining
Mother Earth can never be forgiven!

Nature, and Man

We ought to know, my friend, that
Since Man is an integrated part of Nature,
Nature lies within Man.
Therefore, whatever Nature has achieved,
No matter how high it appears to stand before our eyes,
Still, it is, without doubt, within Man's reach.
For, Nature has endowed us with talents and abilities,
For Man one day the laws of Nature to master!

Nature's Roar

The Corona virus . . .
Nature's roar of discontent –

The boastful Man trembles!

A Cosmic Symphony

The sun has set.
The day wears her evening gown as the
Flickering stars begin dancing in the sky.
Night's mesmerizing song is now heard.

And . . .

Our hearts, attentively, listen to every note
Nature's symphony produces,

While

Our souls join in sacred prayer to offer
Thanksgiving to our Lord
For the cosmic harmony He has established!

The Dawn of a New Era

We
Didn't hear Nature's whispers.

We
Chose to ignore Nature's cries.

We
Even disregarded Nature's roar of her wrath
For all wrongs we were doing
To her,
To life,
To each other.

Then . . .
Silence fell,
An eerie silence,
Carrying with it an invisible virus
That brought
Fear,
Terror and
Death.

Suddenly,
We woke up from apathy's slumber
And rushed forward to repel the invading enemy!

Doctors and nurses,
Police and the army,
Volunteers and priests . . .
All took up arms against a common foe,
All ready to give their lives for their fellow man.

What a glorious manifestation of goodness!
What a magnificent display of brotherhood!
What an apotheosis of divine love!

"*No greater love hath man than laying down his life for his friends.*" (John 15:13)

It is certain
That this is the dawn of a new era,
The birth of a novel world that would be
Kinder
Nobler
Braver
More just and
More loving!

God, my friends,
Works in mysterious ways
To lead us onto the path of righteousness,
The path from which humanity, unfortunately, has
Been led astray!

Spring's Mourning

Anticipating the rebirth of nature,
Onto the fields, I walked the other day,
Hoping to marvel at the outburst of beauty.
On my way, unexpectedly, I met Spring herself just passing by.
Very surprised I was indeed
When, to my dismay, I noticed that her sparkling vitality
Had gone. She looked like an old maid!

No longer was she beauty's incarnation –
Her face was grim; the light in her eyes, dim,
And her lips were tight because of much pain.
Thus, just sadness, desolation, and
Melancholy had remained.

Saddened
By Spring's deplorable appearance,
Cautiously, I approached her, and as
Politely as I could, asked her in this way:

"Oh, ethereal spring,
Whose beauty is admired by the gods and
By all mortals alike,
May I ask you, why in this condition do
I find you?"
Spring,
In desperation, looked at me, and after
Pausing for a while, these words she managed
To utter with a sigh:
"I am mourning the death of my mortal friends

Who so anxiously have been waiting for my coming,
But now that I am here, they, unfortunately, cannot
Witness my blooming!"

It was then
That I detected on her lips a faint smile as
Her eyes turned towards the sky,
Whispering these words at the same time:

"Rest in peace, my beloved friends.
Although you have missed my arrival,
I promise to each of you a flower to grow,
A flower to keep you company
In the eternal spring of paradise!"

*Dedicated to all our brothers and sisters who have lost the battle against COVID-19 and to all those who are still fighting this horrible disease!

Newly Declared Saints

You stood by my side,
tall
unafraid
unyielding –
a tower of
strength!

You were
my doctor
my nurse
my paramedic
my guardian angel.

Ready you were
to oppose the invading virus
to protect me
to cure me
to save my life.

Day by day,
night after night,
vigilant you stood,
depriving yourself
of sleep
of food
of your family.

Little by little,
your efforts paid off.
The enemy retreated.
I recovered.

Jubilant you were,
ecstatic
shouting for joy
for having rescued me
from death's embrace.

I left the hospital,
returning home
to my wife
to my children
to my family.

A few days later,
I tried to contact you
to show my appreciation
for your many sacrifices
and to thank you for offering me
the gift of life.

Alas!
You were not there.
They told me you had passed away,
victim to the disease you had fought against
to cure me.
You had left, they said,
for a better world,
a world where our Lord of love
had reserved a special place for you:
His newly declared saint!

*Dedicated to all my fellow humans who are facing the COVID-19 threat.

We Shall Be Victorious

Here we are, my fellow humans,
fighting for our lives,
struggling to overcome
an unseen enemy.

All over the world, his presence is felt
as it has brought with him agony, tears, and pain.

China, Italy, Spain, and Iran are hard hit,
and many more countries are waiting
their turn to be hit the same.
However, no matter how hard this virus would hit us,
humanity would contiIlnue to survive.

Now, my brothers and my sisters, I call you
to summon all of your courage
and fight in the name of the days that are
still, unborn which wait to see
the dazzling light of life.

Let us, therefore, fight for
our hopes and dreams, without letting
fear reside in our hearts.
For, we have history on our side which has
witnessed the invincibility of Man,
who, no matter what he has done,
under the auspices of our Lord
still remains!

*Dedicated to all my fellow humans who are facing the COVID-19 threat.

Isn't It . . .?

Isn't it ironic
to see the conceited Man
who defies God and abuses nature
and who thinks himself
as the master of the universe,
trembling before a brainless virus?

Isn't it unbelievable
that this deadly and horrible disease
could achieve the unthinkable
to unite humanity?

Isn't it an oxymoron
that fear would succeed
where the mighty love has failed?

Heinous Crimes

On her deathbed,
The fatally wounded Mother Nature bleeds profusely
While the ignominious Man
Drives further his dagger of ignorance into the heart of life;
Thus, unwittingly
Committing at once the most heinous crimes
Of matricide and suicide!

Imploring Nature's Forgiveness

Oh, Mother Nature,
You that were born out of the conglomeration
Of unbounded energy into matter
Under the auspices of the paramount universal Logos
That the harmonious coexistence of opposite forces
Has established by artfully choreographing their coexistence
With the help of the infallible divine will
And were painstakingly interwoven with the assistance of
Mighty space and time!

We humans,
Having realized our abominable crimes against you,
Divine Mother, on our knees, we implore your forgiveness
For our ignorance and our greediness that put you
Through the agony of dying
By disturbing your concordant operation
To satisfy our wretched ambitions, disregarding
Any other forms of life!

The Perfect Democrat

He is the perfect democrat,
for he cares less if one is
a man or a woman,
young or old,
black or white,
rich or poor,
powerful or weak,
knowledgeable or ignorant,
Christian or Moslem.

Who is this ruler that has achieved
this incredible exploit that no man in history
has ever been able to accomplish:
to eradicate discrimination?

Who is this great Caesar
that people kneel before in fear and in awe?

Hail Caesar,
you hateful COVID-19, may
your days be few
and your victims even fewer!

The Hollow Tree

The old tree
Couldn't stand upright anymore.
Age, winds, and storms made it fold,
Condemning it to stay close to
The ground.
Its hollow trunk,
A pitiful sight, one may think,
But it, unceasingly,
Recites the history of the forest.

Oh, how many things Man could learn
If only he was willing to listen to its story!

Roses and Thorns

Wise would be for someone to realize
That God has put the thorns next to the roses
Not to hurt us but to protect the roses' beauty and aroma
For our delight!

Vengeance

Alas!
The poisoning of Mother Earth . . .
Untold suffering shall be cast upon us
And
Upon our children's children

For the blasphemy
Committed against
Our Lord's creation!

In Millions of Ways

In millions of ways, oh Life,
You have emphatically declared to me
That a mortal being I am.

But I, stubbornly, defied your declaration.
Thus, many highways of hope did I build
And many edifices of dreams have I erected
During my fleeting passing through your planes
Of existence, as though I were immortal.

Although my heart knew its mortal nature very well
From the very beginning!

Nature's Bolts

As nature hurls, it bolts at
Whatever stands taller than anything else,
And brings it to the ground.

In the same way, God humbles all those
Who are arrogant, conceited,
Presumptuous, and proud!

Sooner or Later

Man,
Sooner or later, would be called upon
A very hard decision to make,
Either deadly technology to keep
Or his own existence to forsake!

The Leaf

Once, a young green leaf I was
Among thousands of leaves on a tree,
Proud and vibrant among my brothers,
Life's most enthusiastic devotee.

Night and day, on guard I stood,
Vigilant, the foliage I wanted to protect,
Producing oxygen and offering shelter
To every bird that I could detect.

The Spring, though, went fast by
And was followed by the Summer heat.
Hard times, my siblings and l had to face
Till Autumn came and made the heat retreat.

By the middle of Autumn, though,
I noticed my color starting to change.
One by one, my siblings began to fall,
For nature wished her looks to rearrange.

Now, almost all alone, I find
Myself standing on a practically naked wood,
Waiting for the breeze of fate to blow,
Reminiscing the vivid days of my boyhood.

Man ~ God ~ Soul ~ Death ~
Eternity ~ Morality ~
Poetry

Humanity's Moral Pace

Do not wonder, my dear friend,
Why humanity has lost its moral pace.
It is because it has decided to go ahead
Without our Lord's divine grace!

One's Real Life

One's real life dwells in
The depths of his immortal soul.
Thus, no matter what happens to the body,
It hosts her, and
She, unaffected, shall remain.
For, God's spiritual treasures are carried back
Into eternity's domain!

Transcendental Awareness

Purity of heart and mind
Elevates Man's consciousness onto
The sphere of transcendental awareness of
Being: Pure light!

As Strong As . . .

A chain is as strong as its weakest link, they say,
And with that, I whole-heartedly have to agree.
For, it is crucial for us to make an effort:
"Loving each other" to be our sacred decree!

Friendship's Harbor

It doesn't matter if by
An ocean we are separated, my friend,
For, at each sunset, on every wave, my greetings I
Will lay upon you
So that, when the sun rises in your part of the world, they
Will reach you and find in your kind heart a harbor of friendship
To anchor and rejoice!

True Friends

True friends are a treasure,
Deposited in one's heart
From which
One may withdraw any amount
Without ever having to ask!

On Soft Clay

Preferable is for Man, on
Soft clay, his opinions to write.
For, easy to erase them will be
When the truth he finds!

Man, and God

The distance that
Separates Man from God
Can be shortened only
By following the path of Love!

God, and Man

God
Is the only perfect being.
Thus, He is characterized,
Among other things,
By the absence of needs!

Man,
Being imperfect, has many wants.
Thus, if Man wishes to approach God,
First, the plethora of his needs he has to minimize!

The Common Good

The time has come, my loving siblings,
To put the common good above all
And show that we care for each other
To avoid thus bringing Man's downfall!

Aiming at the Common Good

In life,
Love ought to be our motivation;
Humanity, our concern, and
God, our inspiration
If we wish for a better world to be built.
Then, everything we think, say, or do
Should aim at the common good!

Physical and Metaphysical Worlds

The physical and the metaphysical world
Are separated
By the thinnest of membranes.
So, whatever is happening on our side
It is felt in all its intensity by the other.

This is the reason
Why indifferent the metaphysical side cannot stay.
Thus, “they” intervene on our behalf in a plethora of ways:
Influencing our feelings, our thoughts, and our deeds
For the will of our Lord to be implemented and our
Destiny to be fulfilled in the most efficient way.

Religion and Spirituality

If religion is seen as
The wire that connects the soul with
The Divine

Then

Spirituality is the electricity that
Passes through for the dialogue
To commence!

Good Deeds and Prayers

Good deeds, and not fancy words,
Ought to accompany our prayers
If we wish the undivided attention
Of our heavenly father to have!

Crossing the River of Oblivion

"I am very sick",
a dearest friend of mine told me the other day.
"And I think my time has come." She continued with
a bitter smile.

I looked at her with compassion; for, I knew
she was right. I tried to find words to console her,
but none was willing to come to my aide!

Really, what could anyone say in moments like this?

I took her hand into mine, caressed it, and looked deeply
into her eyes, and said:

"My beloved friend,
even the youngest and the healthiest of people that
exist now, would one day find themselves in your
position; for, it is the fate of all us mortals.
Some who are healthy and much younger than you at
the very moment would cross on the other side, because of
an unforeseen event, sooner than they expected."

As I finished my little speech, she turned toward me with
a broad smile and replied:

"How foolish of me to complain about my predicament, when
I knew from the beginning of my life that I am mortal."

Then she slightly pressed her hand into mine as though she wished
to give emphasis to her words, and in a whisper, she added:

"Do not worry my friend, I am ready to face my destiny.
I have no regrets, just gratitude for this marvelous experience,
called life!"

Those were her last words to me.

* This poem depicts a true story.

The Soul's Decision

When the soul prepares herself
A decision to make,
Her eyes fix firmly on the divine first.
For, she has no wish from heaven's plan
To deviate!

Almost Impossible

Always,
The soul that resides in a human body,
Strives with every breath the body takes
To lift it to the land of ideas and ideals by
Giving wings to the dreams and aspirations of her host
And help them become reality according to the laws
Of heavens' decree of harmony and love.

Unfortunately,
The heavy load the flesh carries . . .
Its need for nourishment
Its desires
Its passions
Its ignorance . . .
Renders soul's mission to lift Man from the ground –
Almost impossible most of the time!

Brothers

In this Sleep and Death, defers us

The former on a daily return trip.

The latter, into a permanent one,

Without a chance of return!

*Greek mythology presents Death and Sleep as brothers. The difference is that sleep is temporal and death is a permanent sleep.

The Irony

Oh, future,
You, the unknown dimension of life,
What you have in store for me
I would never know.
However,
I know that among your innumerable
Possibilities there lies ahead on my way
A certainty,
The only certainty that you provide
From which no mortal can ever escape:
Death!

Although, you oh, future,
Have warned me since the day of my birth about
Death's existence,
I never ceased wishing you to advance
At an ever-increasing pace
For the events that beautify life to come
Into existence.

Unfortunately, forgetting that by doing so,
Closer to the lurking death I have come, and victim
To its insatiable appetite am I falling!

What an irony!

The Soul's Consolation

An angel, in his heavenly tranquility, observing the
Lamentations of an inconsolable soul because of its
Upcoming incarceration within the walls of mortal flesh
Turned towards it and calmly said:
"Be patient, dear soul, for manifold your rewards will be in heaven for such a sacrifice!"

Good News

Despair not, my friend,

For

Today's afflictions may turn out to be
The heralds of tomorrow's good news!

A Pen of Inspiration

Charmed
By the pen of inspiration,
The blank sheet of paper
Could no longer resist poetry's advances
And gave in to the temptation
By letting the poem's words to be written on
Its immaculate face.
Thus, transforming itself from an
Insignificant unknown page
Into an important renowned
Manuscript!

Translating a Poem

Translating a poem
Means inhaling the essence of
Its verses,
And
Then exhaling the aroma of
Its very soul!

My Heart's Surrender

Oh, my Lord,
Never was a moment more exhilarating
Than the one when my heart to you I surrendered!

Eternity's Alarm Clock

Death
Is eternity's alarm clock, set to awake the soul
From her temporal lethargic sleep
Of earthly life!

At Every Beat of My Heart . . .

At every beat of my heart, my Lord,
A word of praise turns out to be
An offering of my thanksgiving to life,
But most of all, to glorify Thee!

Surprised

Although Man very well knows
Death is common to us all,
He seems surprised when the time comes
To witness his mortal fall!

The Masterpiece

Each time you envy the beauty of a pearl, my dear friend,
First, you have to think of the oyster's stress, agony, and pain.
For only by going through a lot of suffering
Did the oyster succeed this masterpiece to obtain!

Falling Stars

The souls of my friends, one after the other,
Are leaving the firmament of ephemeral life
For a world unknown
Without revealing their secrets,
And I, in wonder, am asking myself:
"When will my turn come to follow their trajectory
To the world of the blessed
Where the secrets of eternity will be presented to me
In all their glory?"

Death and I

During the funeral of a beloved friend,
I encountered death the other day.
He stood tall,
Imposing,
Majestic,
And not threatening at all.

Encouraged by his look,
I, hesitantly, approached him and dared to ask:

“Why, oh, mighty Death, are you after us humans?”

He looked at me rather surprised and then, smiling, gave me
His reply:

“From where I stand, my friend, it is you who are
After me and not I!”

Ephemeral and Eternal Glory

What a tragedy
to see so many of our fellow men
willingly relinquish their souls’ eternal glory
just to enjoy a few vainly glorious cheers
on the ephemeral plane!

The Lord of the Underworld

The Lord of the underworld
I saw in the streets the other day,
Harvesting terrified souls without mercy.
Trembling because of his scary appearance,
I dared to approach him and asked:
"Tell me, oh, you mighty Lord of darkness,
Why are we mortals so horrified by your sight?"
"Because you ignore what heavens have in
Store for you," was his sharp reply!

Fearless Before Death

A heart, fearless of death,
Is the best defense against the
Lord of the underworld.
For, it deprives him of his
Most lethal weapon:
Terror!

Writing a Poem

"Give me
Words, thousands of words.
I offer my kingdom for words, for I wish a
poem to write. Not any poem, but a masterpiece!" The aspiring
Poet shouted, and then, in a lower voice, added:

"Give me
Nouns, pronouns, adjectives, adverbs,
Determinants, qualifiers, distributives, prepositions,
Infinitives, gerunds, and participles."

"Give me
Verbs, regular and irregular, transitive and intransitive,
Main and auxiliary verbs."

"Now, give me
Tenses, present, past, future, perfect, and conditional tenses.
Active and passive voices included."

"Don't forget to provide me with punctuation as well:
Commas, colons, semicolons, question marks, exclamation points,
Hyphen, and full stops."

"Hurry up, please!
Don't just stand there!
Bring me a chair, a table, and in God's name,
Paper, many sheets of paper of high quality."

"Oh, yes,
I almost forgot! I need a pen, not any pen but
A golden one since this poem is going to remain immortal."

Then he paused for a while and continued his monologue:
“I am all set.
Here I go . . .
I am about to start . . .
Ready to put down the first line . . .”

. . .

Nothing happened.

. . .

He waited for a few seconds.
Still nothing.
Not a single word came to his mind.

“What is wrong with me?” He wondered!
At that moment, he heard a whisper.
He turned around and saw his Muse looking at
Him with pity, and as she approached closer, she said:
“My dear child, if you aspire to be a poet, you
Should approach poetry with awe and not with the arrogance
That you have displayed here. Moreover, open your soul’s eyes
At once to enable them to see the beauty that your mortal eyes
Fail to perceive! You also have to let your heartbeat follow
The rhythm of inspiration which our Lord has put there
For all to use, so as the language of heavens to speak,
Which, to you mortals, as poetry is known!
Remember that fancy words alone
Would never be able to help you with the writing of the poem
Since such is impossible without the intervention of the divine!”

Thus, the Muse spoke and quietly walked away,
Leaving him behind with

His thousands of words piled up before his eyes,
His grammar,
His large table,
His comfortable chair,
His paper of high quality, and of course, his
Golden pen in hand, which, ALAS, had not
Helped him a single word to write!

A Man Without Convictions

Without convictions, a man resembles
An aimlessly sailing boat, in which both the rudder
And the anchor are missing!

A Place of Silence

Desperately, my wandering soul,
A place of silence looks to find.
For, it is yearning the voice of God to hear
And with His Divine Word to bind!

The Instrument

Man is an instrument
In need of tuning,
One that is expected to perform
God's spiritual symphony
On materiality's plane!

The Atheist's Surprise

He was an atheist.
He was proud of it.
Those who believed in the existence of a supreme being
And in the survival of the soul after death,
Were, for him, dim-witted people, worthy only to be
The laughing stock of his "superior intelligence."

He never concealed his denial of God.
He did not need to believe in such a divine being,
Because he knew that he was the superior being, and
As far as the idea of a soul was concerned, there was none.
One dies, and that's it! Game over!

Time passed, and as he was mortal, he died one day.
However, as soon as he was declared dead,
Surprised, the atheist saw himself hovering
All over his inanimate body.
He had no arms, no legs, no head, or any other organs.
Just pure consciousness he was, pure thought,
And pure light.
A sphere of a whitish color he was,
With some sparkling particles
Distributed around its periphery.
In other words, he was a soul.

Confused and bewildered with the situation that the atheist
Himself has now found,
He did not know what to do
And what was coming to him.
In a little while though,

A luminous being approached him,
Wearing the broadest of possible smiles.
The being was emanating love, compassion,
Warmth, and understanding.
As the entity came closer to the atheist, in his mind, these
Words to him were transmitted:
“Do not be surprised, my dear friend, for I am here to
Welcome you and lead you to your creator, whose existence
You have throughout your life so vehemently denied!”

Eliminating Death

What?
I hope you are not serious, my fellow mortal!
Not serious when you suggest that we should
Eliminate death.

How could we?

This is preposterous!

But if you are serious, tell me how we could ever
Exist without the Lord of "darkness".

Come on,
Do not be surprised by my question!
It may sound illogical to you at first, but
Don't you know that life is based on death?

You don't?
How come?

Don't you know that in order for something to live,
Something else has to die?

Let us take the lion for instance, can the lion survive
If another animal doesn't die?
Can an eagle, a python, or a shark thrive if other living organisms
Do not fall prey to their voracious appetite?

Of course, they cannot!

Certainly,
You may think of sheep or of any other herbivorous animal
That does not kill in order to live
But even they eat grass which grows because microorganisms die.
And we, my dearest friend, being omnivorous, eat the sheep
Along with thousands of other animals to ensure our survival.

Yes,
I know,
You would tell me now that you wish to eliminate death
Because you desire us not to die but to keep on living!

Let me tell you something, my dearest friend,
If this is really the reason that prompts you
To wish for death's demise,
You commit the worst of crimes
Because, first, you wish to condemn Man
To an unending suffering, and
Second, you deprive us all of being reborn into eternal life.

You see, my friend,
It would not be good to eliminate death; for, death is
Our liberator and our one-way ticket to immortality!

Eternal Recurrence

I.

Once upon a time,
The Lord of spiritual consciousness was sitting peacefully
On His blissful throne,
Ceaselessly contemplating upon His equilibrium.
T' was the era of no moon, no sun, no stars, no earth,
No oceans, no rivers, just a motionless, timeless
And deathless entity it was, happy with
His existence.

II.

Suddenly, the thought of sacred motion was felt
Deep down in his essence,
Seeking to stir chaos from its core outwardly,
Consequently, separating the light from the darkness
And all the other elements that constitute the Cosmos;
Thus, giving birth immediately to old mighty Time.

III.

When Time, this wizard of celestial art, found himself alive,
His expert hands stretched in advance, wanting to create.
For that, the plastic energy he took, which was everywhere around,
And skillfully and patiently, the Cosmos carved
According to the Logos,
Creating, thus, the nebulae, the galaxies, the stars
And all the other planets.

IV.

Then God looked at Time's creation and marveled its beauty,

But as there was no life to be seen in all of this creation,
The thought of desire was born in God to inhabit every place.
For that, out of Himself, he cut myriads blazing souls
Which, like shooting stars, He sent downwards
To the animate nature.

V.

In this way, to manifestation's cosmic sphere,
The souls were beamed,
Radiating their luminosity to reality's lower planes,
Bringing with them the sacred principles to denser forms of life
As they were passing from the spiritual, the mental and the astral,
And finally, materializing themselves on the physical solid plane
Where life began on earth with God's will and grace!

VI.

Each soul was an ambassador and is of God's will and grace,
A ray of divinity, a guardian of the Holy Law;
Each with a specific mission: to learn, or rather, to remember
How to find the way of return throughout space and time,
And with the Divine, again, to be seen in perfect equilibrium.

VII.

The day I was born, as every man alive,
I found my immortal self-bound to the wheel of Time
That took me around eternity's circumference
In very heavy chains,
Asking to follow obediently the unswerving path of fate:
This endless trip of return where the only constant thing is change.

VIII.

Since then, I have died once and many times after,

But to hold me, death's dark palaces were unable,
As my soul's perpetual desire to follow my destiny
Brought me back to this ephemeral world of fleeting dreams
With a new body, new hopes, and new goals
But always with the same desire.

IX.

Thus, I journeyed back and forth the plains of oblivion,
Choosing the best conditions according to my karma,
Trying to find endlessly the golden middle way
That unmistakably between the extremes is only to be found.
But each time, since from the river of forgetfulness I was drinking,
I was obliged, unfortunately, to start over again.

X.

So, I was born once a king, and another, just a beggar.
In turn, I was born a coward, a hero, a holy man, a vicious man,
A Christian, a Muslim, an atheist, an idolater,
A strong man and a woman,
Healthy and sick, intelligent and witless,
And I was born to love so much the things I once detested,
And to hate passionately the things I once held dear.

XI.

And I was born once to laugh and another, just to cry,
And I drunk successively from joy's cup and that of sorrow's,
And I was born to make friends out of my enemies
And enemies out of my brothers,
And I was born to realize the impossible dreams
And fail the very easy ones,
And I was born to slay and to be slain alternatively
For thousands of years.

XII.

Thus, I lived continuously the extremes of both good and evil,
Striving to find endlessly the balance in my soul
Through the wisdom that was endowed upon me
By the Great Spirit
That, like a beacon, luminous, waits to guide me
To my supreme destiny that GOD for me has traced.

XIII.

So, as I was passing from life unto death, from darkness unto light
With a speed determined by me, I don't put on GOD the blame.
All my lessons have I learned through trial and error
Up to the very last reincarnation in body's mortal temple.

XIV.

Now free, AT LAST, from all earthly desires
And every karmic blame,
Radiating with holiness and glowing with grace,
My immortal soul, HER divine wings unfold and soar
Upwards to the heavens,
White light blazes in perfect equilibrium,
And pure now, to her glorious creator it returns
And with HIM, it UNITES!

Love ~ Friendship ~
Compassion ~ Happiness ~
Hope ~ Fear ~ God

The Fathomless Sea

Fathomless is the sea of love for the one

Whose heart is filled with compassion.

God's Presence

The storm has subsided.
The wind has died out.
The sea has calmed.

The night has passed.
The sun has risen.
Darkness has dissipated.
Fear is gone.
Hope has returned.
My dream is revived.

God gave me another chance;
Another day to live,
Another day to test my wings,
To fly,
To create.

The goal of my life
Appeared before my eyes anew,
Provoking,
Challenging,
Demanding.

I feel God's presence!

My faith is strengthened.
My determination has been reinforced.
My heart rejoices.
My soul is uplifted.

It is certain that, this time,
I would succeed in serving Him better.

For

With the Lord's help,
NOTHING IS IMPOSSIBLE!

* Back in October 2021, I had a serious accident that caused a large Hematoma in my brain, and as a consequence of it, doctors had to perform a long (12") Craniotomy which brought me to the gates of eternity, mute and paralyzed. The doctors did not believe that I could recover. However, God gave me another chance to live. This book is my thanksgiving to HIM!

The Holy Breath

Your holy breath within my chest I carry, oh, God!
The one You did breathe into me on creation's day
That forever makes my heart invincible to feel
And, on no account, allows my soul to go astray!

A Mythical Treasure

There is a mythical treasure
Coming from the heavens above.
Free for all humanity it is.
Its celestial name is "Love"!

Wonder Not

Wonder not, my friend,
Why the buds of love seldom bloom
In Man's heart.

It is because of
The blizzard of indifference that
Hardly ever allows compassion for others
To defrost!

Love's Blooming

If we all let love bloom in our hearts,
Humanity shall be beautified.
If the Word of our Lord we follow,
His holy name shall be glorified!

Defining Love's Essence

All of Man's
Philosophy, literature and poetry
Have failed to define Love.

However,
A single act of sacrifice
Succeeded in designating its essence
Without ever uttering a single word!

Friendship

"Are we really friends?"
My best friend asked me the other day.

"The best there are!" I emphatically replied.

"If we are what you say," he went on,
"How come, you and I refer to our
individual existence as 'I' and 'you' or as
'myself' and 'yourself', and to our possessions as
'mine' and 'yours' as though we are
something distinct from one another?"
Then, in a very serious voice, he added:

"I really wonder about the magnitude of our friendship
which tells us that we are 'one soul inhabiting
two bodies'*."

Hearing all this, I was puzzled. So, after some awkward
Moments of silence, I dared to ask:

"How would you address me then?"

"As me in your body," was his immediate reply!

* The quote, "[O]ne soul inhabiting two bodies" belongs to Aristotle.

Genuine Friendship

You are not a stranger to me,
Neither are you an alien or an unknown.
You are me and I am you in another body.

You are
My soul's double,
My being's twin,
My heart's beats,
My mind's thoughts.

You are
My companion,
My ally,
My friend,
My brother!

I share
Your fears,
Your agony,
Your misery,
Your suffering.
And you share
My hopes,
My joy,
My wellbeing,
My happiness!

Alone, we aren't anymore.
For, you have me and I have you.
Thus, next to each other, we stand

Against all odds
As giant towers of friendship,
Supporting and defending one another,
Asking for nothing,
Offering everything
As we gallantly are toiling to build
Our future’s common path!

Compassion

Compassion is the molten lava
That spewed out of the volcano of love.

The Tree of Compassion

Firmly,
The tree of compassion
Planted its benevolent roots
Into our Lord's Garden of Love,
Expecting to bring forth
The fruits of charity and mercy
Onto the starving humanity!

Compassion, and Love

Compassion and Love,
Are heaven's blessed gifts
That no heart should live without!

An Ounce of Compassion

An ounce of
Compassion in practice,
Rates more than
A ton of love in theory!

Happiness . . .

True happiness is the alignment of one's soul
With the divine Will!

A Humble Advice

If happiness is
What we are after, my dear friend,
Here is my humble advice:

We ought to live
Harmoniously with ourselves,
Our inner self with the outer must be in
Full agreement,
Resolve the conflicts, lingering
In our hearts, and
Free our thoughts from evil.

True Happiness

True happiness is not built on carnal pleasures
But on the moral and spiritual delights
Of the soul.

Once upon a Time

Once upon a time,
Hope, a featherless bird it was,
Which, to escape from despair's land,
Its very own wings did grow
And onto the place of dreams and
Expectations, swiftly flew.

Since then,
Each time one of us feels blue,
Hope flies near him.
And on its aspiring wings of
Optimism and cheerfulness,
Carries him far from the gloomy ground!

Fear

Fear . . .
I saw following me
Like my shadow
The other day.

No matter
How fast I walked
Or towards what direction,
Still, before me, fear I found.

As the hours
Passed by fast, one after the other,
Fear grew taller,
More menacing and
More terrifying.

Knowing not
What to do,
In desperation, my face towards
The sun I turned, praying,
To see Lord's divine light.

It was then that I felt
Lord's light descending upon me,
Setting hope in my heart ablaze;
Thus, making the threatening fear
Once and for all go away!

To Fear or Not to Fear

To the mere mortal, death is something that evokes fear.
To the wise, it is something that is anticipated with hope.

Hope's Burning Flame

Advisable for everyone would be
Hope's bright flame in his heart to keep burning,
To make wishes, fear, and darkness disappear
And to be true to his soul's yearning!

Homeless

Chased by destitution,
Sleeping in the streets, he found himself,
With loneliness and despair as his only
Companions.

In vain, he tried to open hope's sails again;
For, the winds of his dreams had died out
Due to unforeseen events, bad luck, and a dose of
Human indifference.

And now,
He looks at the innumerable streets,
Stretching before his bewildered eyes, in fear,
Wondering if he would ever be able to claim his dream:
The portion of a better future
That he, as a human being, deserves!

The Day You Were Born

The blessed day you were born, my friend, I truly adore
Because it has brought me hope, love, happiness, bliss,
And much more!

If You Ever . . .

If you ever feel lonely
If you ever feel blue
Think of our Lord only
He is thinking of you, too!

Life Is Not . . .

Life is not a banquet or a treat, my mortal friends;
Neither is it a playground for ourselves to enjoy.

It is, instead, a place of strife and deprivation
Where to last, we need God-given talents to employ!

Awake Compassion

Awake compassion!
Do not disregard your destiny's call,
obey it!

Scorch the frantic passions,
Smash the rocks of excess,
And bar the streams of hate!

Awake compassion!
Your face is luminous. Do not turn it
away!
Open the gates of charity,
Trace the path of happiness,
And light mercy's holiest flame!

Awake compassion!
Your noblest hour has come
Humanity's decree to proclaim!

We Are Brothers

Don’t look at me
As though I am an alien or a stranger.
Don’t let the dagger of antipathy
Fly out of your eyes.

I am your neighbor.

Don’t call me a foe, an antagonist, or a rival.
Don’t roll up your mistrustful sleeves for a fight.

I am your friend.

Don’t hold this murderous weapon in your kind hand.
Don’t deny me the right to work, to eat, or to live.

I am your brother.

If destiny willed me to be born
On this side of the frontier line,
If my parents wished me
To wear these clothes
And taught me their own dances,
Do we have to be adversaries?

If fate desired me to speak
This tongue foreign to you
And our skin’s color to differ,
Do we have to be competitors?

If necessity decided for us
To live in this country,
In the North, South, East, or West,
Do we have to be opponents?

If I believe in Jesus,
Jehovah,
Krishna,
Buddha,
Brahma
Or Allah,
If this is my philosophy,
My tradition,
My history
And my culture,
Do we have to be enemies?

No! A million times: no!

Please, look at me with new eyes
And throw away your injurious prejudices.
What do you see but a person like you, who
Wants, desires, and hopes for the same things in life:
Well-being,
Happiness,
A home,
Family,
Some friends,
Some love?

Look:
I walk.
I talk.
I eat.
I sleep.
I dream.
I laugh and I cry.

Just like you.

I'm born,
I grow up,
I learn,
I suffer,
I bleed
And I die.

Just like you.

I'm a father,
A mother,
A brother,
A sister,
A son,
And a daughter.

Just like you.

You see, we are alike.
We are the same.
We are brothers.

Listen to me my neighbor, my friend, and my ally:
I am telling you the truth.
We are the victims of schemes,
Well-planned in advance
By deceitful evil-hearted men, who wished our
Destruction to bring.

They, masters of savage forgery, dividers of mankind
Have tricked us throughout history
With well-orchestrated lies
And with treacherous stories.
These intellectually impotent criminals
Have instilled poison in your heart and mine.

Thus, by cultivating hatred, bitterness, and rage,
They managed to shape us into ruthless foes,
Into merciless enemies,
Into cruel animals.

Please, listen to me! It is true. We are brothers.

Let us, therefore, cross with irresistible will all frontier lines
That the past has erected between us,
Thus, making divisions vanish.

Let us with supreme power, break the bonds of history,
Religion and culture, and run into each other's arms.

Let us uproot from our tormented hearts' thorny mistrust
That was planted there thousands of years ago.

Let us seize ammunition from destructive hatred,
And make war capitulate.

Let us sink the cholera of bitterness
In the affectionate sea of the universal brotherhood.

And finally,

Let us unite and march to higher claims,
To incomparable glory
Where peace can blossom today.
Thus, both of us, my brother, at last, will go to sleep,
Fearless of each other tonight!

*On New Year's Eve of 2016, 2017, 2018, 2019, and 2020, Trifiatis's poem, "We Are Brothers" was celebrated in the Cultural Arts Coalition center in New York where it was performed, along with several other literary works by the author.

Loving Friends

Our friends are
Wingless guardian angels
Who stand by our side, shielding
Our very existence;
Hence, protecting us from any
Foe and evil!

Love and Old Age

Old age . . .
A myth it is, my dearest friends,
A myth, I solemnly, swear.
For as long as we care and love
Forever, young we stay.
This, I emphatically, declare!

Compassionate Hearts

Those who bear love in their hearts
Would never go astray.
For, the Lord dwells within.
Thus, God's love is eternally conveyed.

The Power of Love

Those who truly love their fellow men never die.

For, they live in their friends' hearts.

Thus, death is defied!

The Lords of Terror

I wonder,

Who on earth has designated dictators as the rulers of the world?
Who has given these barbarians the right to rob, rape, and kill?
Who has appointed these evil men as the overlords of humanity?
Who has allowed these monsters to threaten Mankind
with obliteration?
Who has put these savages in a position to intimidate us, our
children, our families, and our countries with nuclear
annihilation?

The answer to all these questions is this: NO ONE!

We are free men,
God-fearing men,
Children of the All-Mighty, who are inspired by
His Love.

Thus,
We must never surrender our GOD-GIVEN rights to these
PARANOIC individuals
Who represent only a few FANATIC citizens of their nations.

For that reason,
We should not stand apathetically still before this abominable
ATHEISTS and
Let them devastate our civilization by imposing chaotic anarchy
and tyranny.

We ought to become vigorously implicated in peace's resurrection
By putting up a gallant fight so as to defeat these brutes and save
Ourselves,
Our children,
Our faith,
Our society,
Our civilization, and
Our beautiful planet!

Wisdom ~ Knowledge ~
Ignorance ~ Opinion ~
God ~ Truth ~ Lies ~ Faith

The Great Truth

Whatever we know,
To God's grace we owe!

Man's Understanding

Man's understanding,
A knee-deep pond it is,
While God's wisdom
Amounts to an abysmal ocean!

Wisdom's Temple

If you, my friend,
Aspire Wisdom's temple to build,
Be patient and, in silence, the cornerstone of it lay:
Self-knowledge!

Truth's Womb

A dialogue with nature, I started,
When I saw beautiful flowers bloom.
The result was to gain understanding
That led me to truth's eternal womb!

Truth, and Man

Truth,
If one knows it, is in reality simple.
Very simple, I might add.
However,
It gets complicated
When . . .
Someone, who ignores it, desperately
Tries to prove that . . .
He doesn't!

Falsity's Tongue

The tongue of falsity . . .
The words of truth can never pronounce!

The Architects

Human knowledge is an edifice
Built by two architects:
Trial and Error!

The Lock of Truth

The secret key with which the lock of truth to unlock,
At last, I found.

Thus,

The chains that kept me ignorant, I shall smash
To let Lord's facts unbound!

Faith

Faith . . .
One's acknowledgment
That one's soul's destiny
Is under God's authority!

True Faith

Entrust
The rudder of your life's boat into
God's hands,
And be certain that it will never sink,
No matter how tempestuous
The sea becomes!

Imploring Divine Wisdom

My Lord,
I pray to You,
You, who are my eternal stalactite,
Imploring Your divine essence
To let Your precious drops of Wisdom,
Upon my craving-for-knowledge-soul,
One after the other, to fall.

For

My earthly stalagmite,
With the passing of time,
Layer after layer of experience and learning,
Towards Your heavenly heights to rise.

Thus,

One blessed day,
Your celestial truth, I will better understand
So that I walk with faith onto Your path of light,
Erring no more!

Knowledge, and Ignorance

Much more preferable it is
For the one who really doesn't know
His ignorance to admit
Than making thoughtless attempts
His competence to show!

Quoting the Wise

The thoughts of many great men he kept repeating,
Believing in that way his wisdom to increase.
But poorer his mind became with each passing day,
Since nothing he said could make his ignorance decrease!

Wisdom, and Man

Yes, it is true.
Man is a friend of Wisdom: A philosopher.
But . . .
Should Wisdom consider Man a friend of hers?

Faith's Harbor

Over many seas of opinions, he sailed,
Seeking the elusive truth to find.
Many decades passed without success.
So, to faith's harbor he anchored his mind!

The Character of the Wise

Moderation
Is the hammer with which
Justice, meticulously, forges the
Character of the wise
On the anvil of virtue!

Thinking

Thinking
Is Man's mental activity aimed at
The initiation of
An inner dialogue with divinity's Nous
In the hope of unlocking life's
Many mysteries!

Wrong Thinking

Wrong thinking
Is the monologue of one's soul
That aims to give license to the self
To do whatever it pleases
Without Divine supervision!

Right Thinking

Right thinking
Is the innate power of the soul
That endeavors to initiate a dialogue with
The Divine to enable one to walk
On the path of righteousness!

Tabula Rasa

No, my child,
Our soul is not a "tabula rasa"
As some men of learning
Want to make us believe.
For,
Our Lord has
Written on her volumes of His wisdom that life's
Experience helps us to retrieve!

The Sun of Faith

When
The sun of faith shines bright,
Human intellectualism
Can clearer discern truth's path.
Provided . . . the vain ego is put aside!

A Myth to Tell

Everyone
Has a myth of life to tell
That none other than him
Can show!

Listen
To him in silence,
And soon, wiser you
Shall grow!

Loving to Learn

If one
Loves to learn
And learns how to love,
Everything in life meaningful becomes!

Transcendental Awareness

Purity of heart and mind
Elevates Man's consciousness
Onto the sphere of
Transcendental awareness of being:
Pure light!

Education

Education
Is the endless fountain
That irrigates the vineyard for learning
Which brings forth the sweet grapes of knowledge
That, with the passing of sensible time,
Produces the exhilarating wine of
Wisdom!

Lovers of Wisdom

What are we but
Inquisitive lovers of wisdom,
Striving to comprehend temporal reality
On the material plane of existence
By closely studying nebulous phenomena
That are mere reflections of transcendental verity
Which, alas, is hermetically sealed
Against our perception
Till the advent of illuminating death?

The Torch

The knowledge of oneself
Is the torch one has to lit
To illumine the path that leads
To God's revelation!

Man, and Reality

Although many eyes see reality,
And as many ears hear its voice,
Few achieve its essence to conceive,
And fewer, with its laws to rejoice!

Vanity, and the Wise

Vanity offered the wise eternal glory among Man,
But he emphatically declined.
Surprised, vanity inquired about the reason
For his rejection which he gave her without much delay:

"Eternal glory among men is something non-existent;
    for, fleeting is the men's world, and fleeting, it will remain,
    no matter how many more millennia men manage
    on this planet to stay.
Moreover, another reason for my refusal I will give you,
    and this, you should keep very well in mind:
    the glory that my soul seeks, you will never be able to offer;
    for, to heaven it belongs, and only heaven can provide!"

The Enlightening Truth

Oh, Divine Truth,
Mountains of prejudices
And
Hills of erroneous beliefs
The mind has to remove
To unearth just a speck of your
Enlightening treasure!

Curiosity

Oh, curiosity,
You, mischievous sibling of wonder,
How many times you have left the main street of
Rationality to venture into the back streets of blind speculation
That, eventually, led you into the dark alleys of confusion,
I would never know.
For that,
A stern warning, I must give you:
Beware of the dead-end streets of the occult that lie in your way.
For, once you enter there, your adventurous self risks a prisoner of
Bewilderment forever to remain!

The Incessant Change

The only permanent thing
In this world we live in
Is change.
Incessantly,
It manages everything
That exists to rearrange!

Gain and Pain

The one who by design hurts his fellow man
Because he yearns something to gain
Must know that he puts his soul into eternity
Through much suffering and pain!

The Brave

Brave is the one who, against all odds,
Over his enemies is able to prevail.
But braver is the one who succeeds in subduing
His passions that his heart impales.

Virtuous and Wicked

For excellence, a virtuous man would strive,
While a wicked one would seek
Iniquity to thrive!

Fame

Nothing is wrong with someone
Who is struggling for fame,
If he is an upright man,
And never puts morality to shame!

Painting and Poetry

Painting is soundless poetry,
Expressed in a myriad of heavenly hues,
While poetry is an audible painting,
Exalting Life in infinite words and sounds!

The Self and the Heart

Oh, my heart,
You and I have been through many stormy as well as
Many peaceful days during our trip through life.

Sometimes,
We have laughed and we have cried so loudly
That we were heard far in the future,
But we have learned that both sorrow and joy
Are interconnected and that one feeling cannot exist
Without the presence of the other.

Moreover,
We realized that the intensity of the feelings,
Produced in both cases, depends on the intensity
Of the feeling caused by its opposite:
The more we suffer, the more we are able to feel joy,
And the greater the joy we feel, the greater the pain
That would follow.

Now,
After so many decades of confrontations on the path of existence,
You and I have become friends.
I do not try to control you anymore, and you do not have many
Reasons to provoke me with your capricious demands.
Thus, it is wise that a truce we finally declare. A truce, that can
Help both of us, my friend, cross in peace the threshold of eternity!

My Odyssey

Here, I am . . .
Retired,
Happy,
Sitting on the relaxing throne of my age,
Reminiscing what I went through in life.
A mere spectator I have now become,
Observing in silence the works of men,
Having no worries
Of career advancement,
Of acceptance,
Of recognition . . .

My only concern is my path to the heavens!

Free at last!
Liberated I feel from all of this soul-disturbing
Situations that preoccupy humans all life long,
In order to enable themselves to survive.

When young,
Things were different . . .
As I wanted to change things,
I roamed the world, visiting all continents but one.
Myriad of dreams I had, each demanding to be realized.

For my part, I did my best despite life's hardships . . .
Starting with the loss of both of my parents
When I was in my early teens.
Then, poverty came, and orphanage for three years.
After that, the struggle for survival intensified –
With me, working and studying.

Being alone at the age of fifteen is not a laughing matter!
Afterwards, I served in the army,
Became a track-and-field long-distance athlete,
Marathons included,
And immigrated to Canada.

Knowing no one over there,
Speaking little English, and having no money . . .
Life was a living hell for a few years,
But slowly things turned around.
For, Canada is a great country.
It gave me chances to work
And the opportunity to study.

I started working during the day,
Going to the university in the evening.
I learned English, French, and German,
Did my undergraduate studies, and then
Completed my post-graduate studies,
Started teaching,
Had my own philosophical TV and Radio program
In three languages at a community station,
Became an author,
Got married,
Had a daughter.

Eighteen years later, I found myself back in Greece . . .
I directed different schools and private colleges,
And in collaboration with professors
From various Greek universities,
I helped organize international congresses on
Philosophy, religion, politics, education, and peace.
Afterward, out of moral obligations,
I was involved in politics, and ran six times

For the Greek parliament and four times, for the
European parliament, with no success.
I did humanitarian work, consoling people,
Visiting hospitals, mental institutions, leper colonies, and
Under the auspices of the Greek Ministry of Justice,
Prisons – high security ones included . . .

Life obliged me to meet people of all walks of life:
Poor men and women that had nothing at all,
Rich and the very rich that had everything.
The illiterate that could not read or write as well as
Famous professors and writers.
Moreover, I met politicians:
Members of the parliament,
Ministers,
Prime Ministers, and
Presidents of different countries.
Also, I came in contact with religious men of
Many denominations:
Bishops,
Archbishops,
Patriarchs, Mullahs
But also, many criminals:
Thieves, rapists, murderers, including some who
Committed fratricide, matricide, and patricide.

I had a harsh and, at times, torturous life
But never a boring one . . .
I was born in an occupied country
During the second WW and lived
The first five years of a civil war that was raging.

If one would ever ask me to live my life again,
My reply would be a thunderous NO!

I could not take it anymore,
Unless . . .
It was to live it again for a higher purpose,
Such as to help achieve world peace.

If one asks me what beautifies life, without hesitation,
I would say: LOVE and LEARNING.

If one makes inquiries about where
I drew the strength to overcome all hardships,
I would say, "my unshakable faith in God,
Who adopted me after the death of my parents,
And my undying love for my fellow man."

If one wishes to know
What the most difficult thing in life is, my reply will be:
To accept life as well as oneself.
Now, to the degree we do not accept life or ourselves,
We suffer!

If one insists on finding out
What is essential for any person in life,
The answer for me is "To know himself, to be truthful to
Himself and to do the best he can by using
The abilities our Lord has provided him with.
That means it is better to be a fine butcher than a lousy doctor!

Finally,
One should never fear death for the simple reason:
None is exempted!
Death for me is a celestial pillow
Upon which the soul rests for a while,
Dreaming of the life to come.
Life much resembles the sea, which, either turbulent or
Calm, has the same depth!

Accept life, and in time, one may learn
How to face death with equanimity!
I am at that point now, with no regrets, other than
I could learn more and
Could have done more in my life.

I thank God for each day of my life.
I, especially, thank Him for giving me more time to live
And produce my new book: *Before the Sun Goes Down*,
After the difficult Craniotomy the doctors had to perform
In order to remove a large brain Hematoma following
The accident I had back in October 2021.

I also thank all those who, directly or indirectly, have enriched
My life's experiences, and have helped
Live this adventure we call "life", including all of you who
Are reading this poem now!

God bless each and every one of you to follow
With determination, courage, love, and faith your
Destiny's path that He for you has traced!

The Author's Quotes

♦ Self-Knowledge ♦

The quest for knowledge starts and ends with the knowledge of the self.

♦ Becoming Wise ♦

Unless one starts thinking for himself, he will never be wise.

♦ The Cornerstone ♦

The edifice of our achievements is built upon the cornerstone that God has laid for us.

♦ A Fearless Heart ♦

Fearless becomes the heart that is armed with love and faith.

♦ Accusing God ♦

Accusing God for one's misfortunes is the epitome of ignorance.

♦ Soul's Aroma ♦

What perfume is to a flower, temperance is to Man's soul.

♦ Love ♦

Love is the vehicle that helps one to fulfill his destiny on earth and in heaven!

♦ An Unblemished Jewel ♦

Love is the unblemished jewel on the crown of humanity.

♦ Life's Coronation ♦

Death is not the end of life but life's coronation.

♦ Breathing and Happiness ♦

Happiness, like breathing, is achieved only by our own efforts.

♦ The Most Precious Gift ♦

The most precious gift God offers to anyone is the dawn of a new day.

♦ Friends ♦

Friends are hosts of one another's souls.

♦ Truth's Melody ♦

Nowadays, our ears have forgotten how the melody of Truth sounds.

♦ A Worthy Life ♦

No life is ever wasted if it serves a higher purpose.

♦ Devoted to God's Love ♦

A heart devoted to God's love would never give shelter to hate.

♦ Temptation's Dagger ♦

Temptation is the sharpening stone of transgression's dagger.

♦ Walls ♦

One cannot enjoy true freedom, unless the walls of his ignorance are torn down.

♦ Courage and Fear ♦

For courage to be born in one's heart, the fear that dwells within must die.

♦ Toiling for Humanity ♦

Whoever works for the good of humanity toils for our Lord.

♦ Inspiration ♦

Inspiration is the roaming of the poet's soul onto divinity's planes of beauty.

♦ A Caring Heart ♦

A caring heart has only its scars to show to prove its concern for others.

♦ Life's Harshness ♦

It is the harshness of life that makes us appreciate more the comfort of it.

♦ Fate and the Soul ♦

Our fate can never be sealed unless the consent of our souls is given.

♦ The Gates of Heaven ♦

The gates of heaven are extremely narrow for a wicked soul but immensely wide for a virtuous one.

♦ The Wounds of Life ♦

The wounds that have been caused by the harsh afflictions of life are the windows that let pass through the understanding's light.

♦ Whoever . . . ♦

Whoever dwells under evil's clouds never sees goodness' sun shine.

♦ God's Residence ♦

In a heart filled with love for one's fellow man is where God resides.

♦ The Tides of Good Fortune ♦

Whatever the tides of good fortune bring, they may take them away with the same ease.

♦ Prudence ♦

Prudence is the guide that may lead one out of the labyrinth of his emotions.

♦ The Unsolved Mystery ♦

Better it is for the living for the mystery of death to remain unsolved.

♦ Soul's Wrinkles ♦

What should worry us is not the presence of wrinkles on our face but the bearing of wrinkles in our souls that may debase divinity.

♦ Moderation ♦

Moderation is the child of just thinking and the grandchild of wisdom.

♦ Not Á La Carte ♦

Each day serves its own dish, regardless of the fact if it is to our liking or not.

♦ Virtue ♦

Virtue is Soul's prelude to heaven's symphony.

♦ We Should Not Forget ♦

We should not forget that for all our achievements God deserves the credit.

♦ Doubting ♦

If one doubts the existence of God, he doubts his own existence.

♦ A Happy Life ♦

Happy is one when his soul dances to the rhythm of divinity's tune.

♦ Tearful Wisdom ♦

The eyes of wisdom stay forever tearful.

♦ Seeking Wisdom ♦

Suffering is the lot of those who seek wisdom; for, interminable is their quest.

♦ Success ♦

Success awaits the one who has embraced his destiny.

♦ The Truth and Lies ♦

Poisonous is the truth for those who feed their souls lies.

♦ Patience ♦

Patience is a wise counselor, a sublime virtue sublime that allows us to reap the fruits of our labor just at the right time.

♦ A Ray of Hope ♦

Even the darkest night of fear is dissipated by dawn's first ray of hope.

♦ Regretting the Past ♦

By wasting time lamenting over past failures, we deprive ourselves of future successes.

♦ The Formula ♦

No surest formula for failure than exceeding the limits of one's capabilities.

♦ Until . . . ♦

Until the ferocious storm of dispute calms down, wise it is to seek shelter in the edifice of silence.

♦ If Man . . . ♦

If the parachute of understanding doesn't open on time, Man would soon find himself in the abyss of mindlessness.

♦ Obsession ♦

One's obsession with material wealth brings his soul impoverishment.

♦ Difficult Tasks ♦

Avoiding to undertake difficult tasks deprives one from achieving great things.

♦ Hecatombs ♦

The long road to happiness is paved with hecatombs of little joys.

♦ The River of Happiness ♦

The source and the estuary of happiness's river lie within our soul.

♦ Guarding Integrity ♦

A vigilant conscience is the most trustworthy guardian of integrity.

♦ Our True Nature ♦

Our true nature is that of love since we all are God's children.

♦ What Is a Poem? ♦

A poem is the display of the soul's beauty painted in divine hues.

♦ In God's Hands ♦

Let us put our fate in God's hands; for, it is certain that it will never be betrayed.

♦ Fruits of Wisdom ♦

The only fruits that have no specific season to ripen are those of wisdom.

♦ Peace in Our Hearts ♦

When our good deeds exceed in number our misdeeds, our hearts find peace.

♦ The Heart and Its Desires ♦

A million excuses will the heart find to fulfill its countless desires.

♦ Excessive Pleasure ♦

Without fail, each excessive pleasure has a price to pay in full.

♦ God's Grace ♦

An arid land would Man's heart be, if it is not irrigated by God's grace.

♦ Life ♦

Life is the perpetual dialogue between God's ideals and creation.

♦ The Healer ♦

Hope is the healer that nurses our ailing dreams back to health.

♦ Truly Rich ♦

Truly rich is the one who doesn't possess anything, yet he asks for nothing.

♦ Integrity's Mission ♦

Integrity is the moral obligation in safeguarding the sanctity of our being.

♦ Great Exploits ♦

If one desires to achieve great exploits, he must be ready to make great sacrifices.

♦ Heart's Throne ♦

Vices enthroned in one's heart keep the Man from God apart.

♦ Sadness and Gladness ♦

Sadness is the gaiety of grief. As for gladness, it is the sobriety of happiness.

♦ Ignorance, Knowledge, Wisdom ♦

Ignorance shouts. Knowledge speaks. Wisdom whispers.

♦ Grief's Garden ♦

The most fertile soil for the tree of Wisdom seems to be found in the garden of grief.

♦ Weaving Wisdom's Cloak ♦

Experience is the maiden that assists knowledge in weaving the cloak of Wisdom.

Epilogue

About Demetrios Trifiatis

Demetrios Trifiatis, was born in 1944 in a small village in Greece, some three hundred kilometers from Athens. He is the third child of a poor family of eight children. At that time, Greece was occupied by the Nazis and the Fascists. The oppressors left later that year. It was then that a Civil War broke out that lasted till 1949. When the war was finally over, the country was devastated and, because of their political convictions, the hearts and minds of the people were filled with bitterness, rage, and hate that lasted for decades.

The author learned his first letters at the primary school of his village. Unfortunately, at the age of ten, he lost his father, and at the age of fourteen, his mother. Having no choice, he was sent to an orphanage for three years. After completing his early education there at the age of fifteen, he went to Athens where he started working in the day and attending school in the evening.

Wishing to enter a university but not having the means to support his studies, the author legally immigrated to Montreal, Canada where he started working and studying at the same time. The road to obtaining a degree was not easy; so, he had to make many sacrifices as he did not know anyone over there. However, after four years, he completed his undergraduate studies in Philosophy at Concordia University and then continued his studies at Université de Montreal where he completed his postgraduate studies, also in philosophy. His doctoral thesis is on the philosophy of Heraclitus of Ephesus. The author studied English, French and German, and upon the completion of his studies, taught in Canada where he stayed for eighteen years. During those years he got married and had children, and became a Canadian citizen.

Demetrios Trifiatis has written and published short stories, wrote the libretto of a historical oratorio called "Heroes" that was presented in Montreal under the auspices of the Greek Ministry of Culture. He created a radio and a television program of philosophical and historical content that run for two years. Both programs were very popular. The television program was presented by him in three languages: Greek, English and French; so, he became known as the professor who speaks many languages.

He has authored two other books of poetry: *Whispers of Inspiration* and *Lessons Life Taught Me*. In addition, he has co- authored *An Aegean Breeze of Peace*. It must be noted that in his poetry the author expresses his agony concerning the future of the present world and makes suggestions of how the ills of this world could be healed. He focuses on ethics and metaphysics which are the fields of his philosophical specialty. Today, he is considered to be an internationally acclaimed poet whose poetry has been translated into several languages and has been used in schools and by organizers of peace events around the world, including Germany, England, India and the U.S.A.

The author was a member of the Canadian Philosophical Association, and became the Secretary General of the Greek International Center of Philosophy and Interdisciplinary Research after his return to Greece. In that capacity, he helped to organize a number of international symposia on philosophy, religion, education, and politics in collaboration with professors from various Greek universities. He became the Academic Director of different private schools and colleges, and out of moral obligation, has run six times for the Greek Parliament and four times for the European Parliament. During that period, he came in contact with many politicians, including prime ministers and presidents as well as religious leaders of different denominations. His experiences in these areas unravel in more detail in his poem “My Odyssey”.

Demetrios Trifiatis has been involved with humanitarian organizations, having participated in peace events, including that of Malta in 1989 when President Bush of the United States and the Soviet Secretary General Gorbachev had met. The author represented a peace movement of Greece and was a member of the presidium of the world peace movements where he read his poem, “We Are Brothers II” which was received positively, and as a result of it, he was invited to visit several countries. Later on, the same poem has been taught in schools and was used in peace events around the world and has won numerous distinctions.

Apart from the peace movement, the author voluntarily visited hospitals, mental institutions, leper colonies, as well as prisons – high security prisons included. These undertakings were done under the auspices of the Greek Ministry of Justice. He also offered free English language lessons at his church. In fact, the author has been working throughout his life toward alleviating the suffering of his fellow humans in any possible way, consoling for over forty years the relatives of those who have left this world for a better one. In his efforts in this direction, the writing of this book takes a particular significant place.

Demetrios Trifiatis, who is approaching his eighth decade on the planet, has travelled extensively around the world, having visited four out of the five continents. He still dreams, God willing, of visiting the fifth continent as well. Apart from Greece where he lives presently and Canada where he lived for eighteen years, he has stayed more than two years in the UK, and for several months, in Denmark, mainland U.S.A., Hawaii, China, and New Zealand. He loves learning languages. He speaks Greek, English,

French, German, and has studied Danish, Italian and Chinese. Presently, he is retired. He writes poetry and gives speeches. He tends to a garden of his creation and loves to grow flowers that he adores.

Notes from the Editor

Demetrios Trifiatis is a celebrated multi-lingual poet online, in Greece, in the U.S.A.; in fact, globally. A large number of his poems have been translated into various languages, including Arabic, Spanish, Indonesian, Serbian, Bengali, and Filipino. His poem, "We Are Brothers", has been added into the Senior High school curricula by the German Association of Teachers of English Language in Germany with the author's permission. In addition, a 9-page long test was prepared for the students. The same poem, which had won the first prize at a peace festival in India, has been cited at peace events around the world. Numerous humanitarian organizations have used the same poem as well as other poems of the author for their events.

In 2019, the author was invited by Duke University in Durham, NC as a Keynote Speaker and featured poet. He was eagerly received by this noted American university, to the extent that his poetic work was compared to that of Walt Whitman. During his visit, Trifiatis recited many of his poems, among them, "World Day Against Racism" which Duke University used to produce a documentary on love.

On New Year's Eve of 2016, 2017, 2018, 2019, and 2020, Trifiatis's poem, "We Are Brothers" was celebrated in the Cultural Arts Coalition center in New York where it was performed, along with several other literary works by the author. In 2016 and 2017, his numerous poems were recited along with selected poetry by Emily Dickinson. In his third solo poetry book, *Before the Sun Goes Down*, the poetic constructs as well as philosophical quotes by the author speak for themselves when his wide-range influence is concerned.

Whenever creative writings are concerned – those of mine included, a professional editor comes across challenges on the surface or in the content of a manuscript. While some editing professionals prefer to re-write an authentic work, I, as a seasoned editor of a large variety of written constructions, routinely seek a middle ground; for, I view and honor the authorial voice as the utmost vital aspect of any creatively composed text. The essence of that voice must under all circumstances be conveyed authentically to the readership – any and all poetic licenses included.

It seems imperative to emphasize at this point one dominant aspect of Demetrios Trifiatis' writing style; namely, his approach to the mainstream rules on word order. As with all of his published poetic offerings, he moves away from the English conventional order of words also throughout this book. Poems such as the following, thus, do not constitute at all a rarity in the collection before you:

Life's Secrets

Once, I asked mysterious life
All her secrets to reveal.
Since I didn't get any reply,
Her lips . . . I had to unseal!

Another example, as the one below, shall suffice to adequately and efficiently demonstrate the matter of focus:

Nature's Secrets

Listening attentively to nature's whispers,
The secrets of eternal life, I was taught
Secrets, hidden in every being, existing
That my perplexed mind forever has them sought!

With regard to the use of "standard word order in English", the reader of Demetrios Trifiatis would be best served if s/he could rise above the expectations that the ordinary users of the English language impose upon us across the board. While in that reading mode, dear reader, you might want to allow yourself to reach beyond the boundaries that literary theorists and rigid editors prescribe for specific language uses. By doing so, you would be able to amiably embrace the author's sophisticated thought processing and delivery of eloquent content.

hülya n. yılmaz, Ph.D.

Professor Emerita, Liberal Arts ~ The Pennsylvania State University
Director, Department of Editing Services at
Inner Child Press International

Other Books

by

Demetrios Trifiatis

Whispers
of
Inspiration
Demetrios Trifiatis

Lessons
Life Taught Me
Demetrios Trifiatis

An
Aegean Breeze of
Peace
by
Demetrios Trifiatis
and
hülya n. yılmaz

Inner Child Press

Inner Child Press is a publishing company founded and operated by writers. Our personal publishing experiences provide us an intimate understanding of the sometimes-daunting challenges writers, new and seasoned, may face in the business of publishing and marketing their creative "Written Work".

For more information:

Inner Child Press

www.innerchildpress.com

intouch@innerchildpress.com

Inner Child Press International

'building bridges of cultural understanding'

202 Wiltree Court, State College, Pennsylvania 16801

www.ingramcontent.com/pod-product-compliance
Lightning Source LLC
LaVergne TN
LVHW010057170826
845678LV00012B/2156

* 9 7 8 1 9 5 2 0 8 1 9 6 5 *